RIVERS

Rivers

RONALD RUSSELL

DAVID & CHARLES
Newton Abbot London North Pomfret (Vt)

British Library Cataloguing in Publication Data

Russell, Ronald
  Rivers.
  1. Rivers
  I. Title
  551.4'83   GB1203.2

  ISBN 0-7153-7473-7

Library of Congress Catalog Card Number 78-52169

© Ronald Russell 1978

Set by Trade Linotype Ltd, Birmingham
and printed in Great Britain
by Biddles Limited, Guildford
for David & Charles (Publishers) Limited
Brunel House   Newton Abbot   Devon

Published in the United States of America
by David & Charles Inc
North Pomfret   Vermont 05053   USA

CONTENTS

(*frontispiece*) The Derbyshire Wye

ACKNOWLEDGEMENTS

I would like particularly to thank Mr Guy Hemingway, for allowing me to make use of his researches into the crossings of the Trent. I am also grateful to officers of the various Regional Water Authorities, the North of Scotland Hydro-Electric Board, the Kew Bridge Engine Trust, and to Mr Charles Hadfield and Dr Ben Barr. The appendix originally appeared in *Our Waterways*, published by Murray in 1906.

Acknowledgements are due to the following for illustrations: British Tourist Authority (frontispiece and pp 22, 28, 58, 109, 124, 128, 133, 166), Cambridge University Dept of Aerial Photography (p 10), North of Scotland HEB (pp 40, 153), Kew Bridge Engine Trust (p 42), Anglian Water Authority (pp 46, 48), Cambridge University Library (pp 62, 64), Charles Hadfield and David & Charles (p 75), Cambridgeshire Collection (p 90), Humber Sloop & Keel Preservation Society (p 92), British Waterways Board (pp 96, 97), King's Lynn Library (p 88), Nottingham Library (p 106), Birmingham Library, Sir Benjamin Stone collection (p 123) Royal Society for the Protection of Birds (p 135), Tamaris Askem (pp 139, 142), St Neots Library (p 146), Welland & Nene River Division (p 147 upper left), Radio Times Hulton Picture Library (pp 180, 182 lower). The remaining photographs were taken by myself, or by Nigel Bloxham from books and prints in my possession. The books include *Rivers of Norfolk*, by James Stark (1834), Mr & Mrs S. C. Hall's *Book of the Thames* (1859) and H. R. Robertson's *Life on the Upper Thames* (1875).

Finally I am (as always) indebted to my wife Jill, and to Adrian Russell and Simon Ross for help in various ways.

1

RIVERS IN THE LANDSCAPE

Rivers give shape and character to landscape, focus and reason for settlement, avenues for trade, provision for sport and recreation, inspiration, usefulness and delight. Without water there can be no life; of all our cities, towns and villages it is those upon or near to water that have endured. And if there is an essential quality to English landscape perhaps it is that seen by William Cowper, living in Buckinghamshire; 'all flat and insipid', he described it. But in this very ordinary countryside he could see what mattered:

> Here Ouse, slow winding through a level plain
> Of spacious meads, with cattle sprinkled o'er,
> Conducts the eye along his sinuous course
> Delighted.

He saw the elms screening the herdsman's hut, the hedgerows, the church spires, the villages, all held together, as it were, by the river glittering in the sun.

Let us now look a little further, and try to answer some questions. What part have rivers played in the patterns of life in our communities? How have river-crossings shaped the development of countryside and towns? What crafts and occupations have grown up on riversides, and what do rivers mean to those interested in natural history, literature, painting? What do their names tell us about them? How has man come to control them, and what effect may this control have on our—and their—future?

First of all, then, landscape—or riverscape if you prefer. Water has no choice but to flow downhill, and the attraction of river scenery lies in the many different ways in which it does so. Compare the scenery of Welland with that of Wye. The Welland, rising in the hills near

7

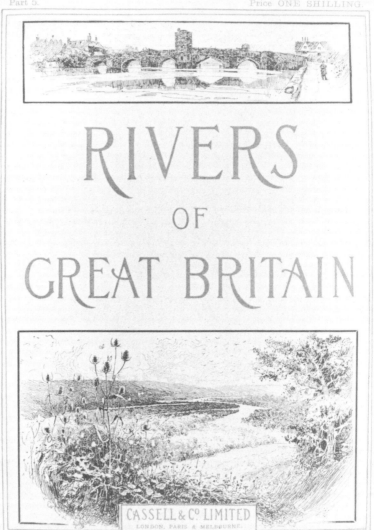

Cassell's Monthly Publication *Rivers of Great Britain*, 1890-91. 'The work is one', said the *Saturday Review*, 'which is good to remind one of past holidays, and to suggest future ones, full of delightful pictures of hill and dale, of picturesque village and quiet town, of stately cathedral and ruined castle'

8

Naseby, flows gently eastwards through amiable pastoral scenes, pottering along through Rockingham and the Vale of Catmose, passing near the famous quarries of Collyweston, Barnack and Ketton, to be crossed by the Great North Road and arrive in the fine old town of Stamford. For a few miles more it is a friendly little river; then the small hills and woods recede, the flat fields stretch away and the settlements string themselves along the riverside as if it were a frontier. After the Deepings, the land sinks and the river seems to rise sharply, its banks now towering above the fields. Above Spalding, once an inland port, much of the flow is taken off and channelled around the town. Then, again embanked and soon joined by its tributary, the Glen, the Welland is guided by the work of engineers to Fosdyke, the Wash and the sea.

The Wye could hardly be more different. It rises on Plynlimon, the 'huge and dreary hill' where Owen Glendower established a head-quarters in the reign of Henry IV. For the first few miles it runs through boggy, marshy ground, collecting an occasional tributary stream; then the terrain changes and the water runs clear and flashy over a gravelly, stony bed. Descending, it carves out its valley southwards through the hills, but always edging its way towards the west. At the river-crossings small towns have grown up: Langurig, Rhayader and the village of Newbridge. The landscape is gently pastoral, with rolling hills. South of Newbridge, the Wye is joined by the Ithon, soon after that river has escaped from Llandrindod Wells whose sprawl of red brick sits inappro-priately in Radnorshire. A strong-running river, the Wye collects the Irfon and the Llynfi and loops to head eastward by the border town of Hay—now containing the world's biggest second-hand bookshop—and swings into a series of meanders through the Herefordshire plain. It is a feature of the townscape of both Hereford and Ross. Below Ross, through what is now the Lower Wye Valley, the river has worn its way through a series of different rocks, with cliffs rising on the outer curves of the loops of its course. Here is some of the finest river scenery in Britain, at Coldwell Rocks, Symond's Yat and Seven Sisters Rocks. At Monmouth the valley widens, the hills recede to form a circle around the small town where Henry V was born and Monnow joins Wye. One hill only, the Kymin, crowned by Britain's single naval temple—it was this area that supplied the timber for many of the ships under Nelson's command—stands in the foreground. The valley closes in; the Wye has cut its way through the Old Red Sandstone, and the Cistercians built their abbey at Tintern on the rich soil the river brought down. Then come the drama of the Wyndcliff and Wintour's Leap, Chepstow

Castle, and the mud flats through which the channel winds to the Severn and the Bristol Channel.

In the lower reaches of the Welland the land has subsided, while the river runs above our heads as we walk along outside the embankments. In its lower reaches, the Wye has forced its way downward through the rock and we have to climb to the top of the valley cliffs to reach the level of the river as it once was. Some of the abandoned meander loops in the Forest of Dean are 400ft above the present river.

Welland and Wye provide outstanding examples of the way in which a river can affect and relate to the landscape through which it flows. The

The River Welland at Deeping St James, Lincolnshire

The Wye at Symond's Yat, from Samuel Ireland's *Picturesque Views on the River Wye*, 1797. Note the four horses towing on the left of the picture. The buildings on the other side are iron forges

Welland, incidentally, is a great coarse-fishing river, while the Wye is one of the finest salmon rivers outside Scotland.

There is no such thing as a typical river, but an examination of the highest reaches of a river is a great help to understanding something of the effect of moving water on the landscape through which it flows. Read the words of one of the earlier popularisers of geology, Lord Avebury:

We surprise the river at its very commencement: we can find streamlets and valleys in every stage; a quartz pebble may divert a tiny stream, as a mountain does a great river; we find springs and torrents, river-terraces and waterfalls, lakes and deltas, in the space of a few square yards, and changes pass under our eyes which on a larger scale require thousands of years. And as we watch some tiny rivulet, swelling gradually into a little brook, joined by others from time to time, growing to a larger and larger torrent, then to a stream, and finally to a great river, it is impossible to resist the conclusion that . . . even the greatest river valleys and plains, and the general configuration of the land, though their origin may be due to the initial form of the surface, are due mainly to the action of rain and rivers.

And, as the upper reaches are miniatures of the whole, so smaller rivers are often miniatures of greater, provided that they run through similar terrain. On the larger rivers, however, the effect of the controlling hand of man is often evident and it is only in times of flood that we can sometimes obtain a sense of how things once were.

Of all river features, the waterfall is the most enthralling, although, statistically, the waterfalls of Britain are unimpressive compared to those of countries where nature operates on a massive scale. Eas Coul Aulin— the Gaelic word *eas* means waterfall—at nearly 700ft is the highest in the United Kingdom; it is near the head of Loch Glencoul in Sutherland and can be reached by boat or on foot, but is not accessible by car. Far better known are the Falls of Clyde, tourist attractions since the late eighteenth century. Now it is only twice a year when the falls can be seen in their full force, as for some fifty years much of the water of the upper river has been taken off for hydro-electric power. As with the Severn Bore, you have to make enquiries beforehand, only, with the Clyde, it is the hand of man that closes the valve to release the natural flow down the falls of Bonnington, Corra Linn and Stonebyres. The Falls, within a few miles of Lanark, provided delight and amazement to early travellers and artists in search of the picturesque. Seats were considerately placed in the best viewing positions; a pavilion was built at Corra Linn, with a mirror on the wall inside to enhance the effect of the spectacle. It made Dorothy Wordsworth laugh when she visited it and saw the fall above her head, 'reflected in a mirror and bustling like suds in a washing tub'. Being comparatively easy to reach, the Falls were popular with landscape painters; Turner painted two oils of Corra Linn, and Paul Sandby, Jacob More and Francis Nicholson were others whose views can be seen in major art galleries.

On the Tay are the Birks of Aberfeldy and the three falls of Moness, with a distance of about half a mile from the top of the highest to the bottom of the lowest, near the village and General Wade's famous bridge, built by William Adam over the river in 1733 when the General was busy suppressing the Jacobite supporters in the Highlands. Robert Burns vividly described the Birks:

The braes ascend like lofty wa's,
The foaming stream deep roaring fa's,
O'erhung with fragrant spreading shaws . . .

There is now a Nature Trail to the falls and various other tourist aids and attractions in the neighbourhood, but it remains a dramatic and enchanting place.

Like the Falls of Clyde, the Falls of Foyers, on the River Foyers to the south of Loch Ness, have been affected by the use of their water for hydro-electric power. There are two falls, the top one 30ft high and the lower about 90ft. Robert Burns came here also, in 1787:

Among the heathy hills and ragged woods,
The roaring Foyers pours his mossy floods,
. . .

The verse is not memorable but the sight certainly was. It has been described as 'the most magnificent, out of all sight and hearing, in Britain . . . it is worth walking a thousand miles for one hour to behold the Fall of Foyers'. Nineteenth-century tourists visited the Falls by steamer from Fort Augustus. Black's *Picturesque Tourist of Scotland* tells us that pony carts awaited the arrival of passengers, conveying them to the head of the lower fall where there was a footpath. By this means, ladies could view the Falls without fatigue; the cart cost ninepence or a shilling and the tender to and from the steamer a further sixpence. Conscientious as always, Black gives the traveller a timely warning: 'A man who calls himself a guide tries to levy a toll on the visitors; but as he is of no use, the road being unmistakable, he is entitled to nothing.'

Among the many waterfalls in Scotland are three with the same name— Grey Mare's Tail. The highest is in Dumfries about 8 miles from Moffat, where the Tail Burn drops 200ft down to Moffat Water. The surrounding area now belongs to the National Trust of Scotland: visitors should be wary of the wild goats. The name of the fall is appropriate; the water descends in a scatter rather than a continuous torrent. Around 1811 a man trying to climb up the rock-face fell to his death. 'Long afterwards,' says Black, 'portions of his dress might be seen attached to some of the inaccessible points of the rock.' There is a grave below the waterfall, a hollow called Giant's Grave and nothing to do with this particular casualty.

Of the two other Grey Mare's Tails, one is a 100ft fall on the Crichope Burn, near Thornhill, also in Dumfries, and the other is a 60ft fall in Kirkcudbright.

The Birks of Aberfeldy, engraved by W. Richardson after a painting by
D. O. Hill

Across Scotland, in Perthshire, where Lowlands and Highlands meet, are the Falls of Bracklinn on the Keltie Burn, a succession of torrents, rapids and linns (pools), where 'above a chasm where the brook precipitates itself from a height of at least 50ft there is thrown a rustic footbridge, of about three feet in breadth, which is scarcely to be crossed by a stranger without awe and apprehension'. The River Leny cuts down from the Perthshire Highlands to Callendar. Salmon leap up the Falls of Leny on their way northward to spawn; Ben Ledi looms to the west and the main road, the A84, leads around Loch Lubnaig through Strathyre Forest to Lochearnhead. This is the countryside of *The Legend of Montrose*.

In mountainous Wales, as in Highland Scotland, the very configuration of the land makes the waterfall an integral part of the scene, sometimes defeating even the most enthusiastic builder of roads. But, again as in Scotland, many of the Welsh waterfalls have had their flow diminished by demands for hydro-electric power or have become tourist attractions with admission fees and car-parking problems. The highest of them—and perhaps the most spectacular—is Pistyll Rhaeadr which falls some 250ft down steep rock near the headwaters of the Afon Rhaeadr, a tributary of the Tanat. It is accessible from the end of a road that strikes out into the hills north west from Llanrhaeadr-ym-Mochant and gives up at Tan-y-Pistyll, just below the falls. More popular are the so-called Swallow Falls near Capel Curig, above the junction of Llugwy and Conwy. 'First there are a number of little foaming torrents,' wrote George Borrow, describing the falls, 'Then come two beautiful rolls of white water, dashing into a pool a little way above the promontory; then there is a swirl of water round its corner into a pool below on its right, black as death and seemingly of great depth; then a rush through a very narrow outlet into another pool, from which the water clamours away down the glen.' Car parks, cafés, fencing and wire have all appeared in later years, and the Capel Curig area in the summer months is usually one enormous traffic jam. The same is true of Betws-y-Coed and the nearby Conwy Falls. The whole of this area—the whole of Snowdonia—is under the greatest pressure from tourism in the holiday season.

The waterfalls of England, although many of them are easily accessible, do not come under quite such intense scrutiny. It is true that, at High Force on the Tees, where the water sweeps down, falling 70ft over an outcrop of the Great Whin Sill, there is an admission fee at the entrance to a path leading through the wooded banks, and a hotel with a car park. But the hotel is whitewashed and unpretentious (it was once the Duke of Cumberland's shooting lodge), the car park is discreet,

(*left*) High Force on the Upper Tees; (*right*) Cauldron Snout,
England's greatest waterfall, on the Upper Tees

there is no collection of signposts or souvenir shops. Nevertheless, about
100,000 people a year visit the spot. The building of a reservoir above
the longer cascades of Cauldron Snout, 6 miles upriver, means that the
chances of seeing High Force in full glory, when the water falls down
two channels, or even covers the central spur of rock, are remote, if not
impossible. In a hard winter, however, it will still freeze solid. The pool
beneath the Force is said to be about as deep as the fall is high.
Nathaniel Spenser, writing in 1773, said that those who had seen the
Nile cataracts or Niagara Falls would be reminded of them by High
Force, and that those 'whose stations in life hinder them from travelling
into foreign countries to visit these natural curiosities may see them all
here in epitome'.

The Tees, in this vicinity, is the boundary between Durham and
Yorkshire. There are some fine waterfalls in Yorkshire. On the Ure are
the three great slopes of Aysgarth Falls. Fossdale Beck, a tributary of the
Ure, has Hardraw Force; the beck tumbles over a projecting limestone
cliff and it is possible to walk around the back of the falling water. There

16

are falls on the Wharfe, 'a swift and speedy stream,' Camden described it, 'making a great noise as it goeth, as if it were froward, stubborn and angry'. This river drops 600ft in its first ten miles. On the upper reaches of the Wharfe there are few really old bridges, owing to 'a wonderful inundation of waters' in September 1673, which swept away six bridges between Kettlewell and Otley and carried away wooden mills 'whole, like to a ship', and all the crops and cattle near its banks. The Falls are near Linton; about four miles below is the narrow gorge known as the Strid. Here, according to the legend as told by Wordsworth, the young heir to the Romilly estates, the 'Boy of Egremond', was one day hunting and tried to leap across the rushing waters:

> He sprang in glee, for what cared he
> That the river was strong and the rocks were steep?
> But the greyhound in the leash hung back,
> And checked him in his leap.
> The Boy is in the arms of Wharfe,
> And strangled by a merciless force;
> For nevermore was young Romilly seen
> Till he rose a lifeless corse.

Nearby are the ruins of Barden Tower, dating from 1485, and a few miles below, by a bend in the river which can be crossed by stepping stones, is Bolton Abbey, said to be founded by Alicia de Romilly, mother of the Boy of Egremond. With its rivers, dales, moors and hills, its caves, abbeys and traditions of rural craftsmanship, North Yorkshire is wonderful countryside, although again under pressure from tourists and coach parties. Recall, however, the words of two country-loving divines, the Reverends Samuel Manning and S. G. Green, writing about a hundred years ago about this area in holiday times·

He who would be free from excursionists, with their loud talk, their demonstrative ways, their baskets and their bottles, must go another time; but even in these holiday-hours there is much to interest. The 'trippers' may be an interruption to the dreamer, an annoyance to the sensitive; but it is good that people whose lives are usually so hard-pressed and monotonous should have the means of ennobling enjoyment within easy reach; and though occasionally there may be an element of roughness or even intemperance in their recreation, we should be unjust were we not to record our impression, that the free access to hill and moor, to fine scenery and pure air, has its part in checking those vices which spring up like evil weeds in the unwholesome dwellings of a crowded population.

Greta Hall and Keswick Bridge. Robert Southey lived in the Hall for several years. Engraved by E. Francis after a drawing by William Westall

Let us agree with the comment—after all, it bears the impress of the Religious Tract Society—while still making allowances for the changed circumstances, many of today's 'trippers' being wealthy folk from foreign parts, and accepting the domination of the motor car. It applies also to the Lake District, where water and mountains compete in attracting the visitor. Wordsworth's own *Guide to the Lakes* is still the best introduction to the region. The rivers themselves he felt to play only a contributory part to the majesty of the district, even the larger being, in the mountain and lake country, 'rather large brooks than rivers'. He commented on the clarity of the water flowing over rock or blue gravel, 'which give to the water itself an exquisitely cerulean colour: this is particularly striking in the rivers Derwent and Duddon, which may be compared, such and so various are their beauties, to any two rivers of equal length of course in any country. The number of the torrents and smaller brooks is infinite, with their waterfalls and water-breaks;' he continues, but then disappointingly, 'and they need not here be described.' Wordsworth devoted thirty-five sonnets to the Duddon and celebrated the Derwent frequently. Southey lived at Greta Hall at Keswick for forty years, becoming as much of a tourist attraction for the literate as the mountains and lakes themselves. He perpetrated the well known verses on the Falls of Lodore on the Watendlath Beck which tumbles down to Derwentwater. More impressive than the Lodore Falls is Scale Force, 'the loftiest and noblest, as well as the most secluded of the lake waterfalls', on a stream falling into the western side of Crummock Water. There are plenty more, including Colwith Force, Airey Force and the cascades on Sour Milk Ghyll in Easedale. In addition, there is the lofty waterfall, Dungeon Gill Force, on the south-east side of Langdale Pikes, described by Wordsworth, whose 'Idle Shepherd Boy' passed over the bridge of rock, as have many older and less agile folk since.

Elsewhere in England there are few waterfalls of any considerable height. Devon has the Lydford Cascade, where a tributary brook from Dartmoor falls about 100ft to the River Lyd. This fall has been called 'the Woman in White' and visitors have been warned to keep clear of her embrace. 'I have myself seen a rash visitor borne away senseless, after being swept down the fall against the cruel rock which, midway, momentarily checks its force', reported J. L. W. Page, authority on the rivers of Devon. Then there are the cascades on the East and West Lyn, which merge at Watersmeet and emerge at Lynmouth where the river, swelled with floodwaters draining off Exmoor, during a night of extraordinarily heavy rainfall in 1952, destroyed much of the little seaside town.

Less known, perhaps, are the falls of South Wales, in country off the better-known tourist tracks. Not far from the old mining areas are the upper reaches of the Afon Nedd (River Neath) and the Afon Mellte; there are also the spectacular Henryd Falls on the Nant Llech as it makes its way down to the Tawe. And there are plenty of lesser torrents pouring down the hillsides of the steep South Wales valleys where rivers, roads, and, a few years ago, railways and canals jostled each other on their way to the ports of the Bristol Channel.

In waterfalls, rivers impose themselves dramatically upon the landscape. Nature being, on the whole, a levelling agent—and man, on the whole, likewise—what we have is in general less impressive than what we have lost; the waterfall that once coursed over Malham Cove would have been mighty indeed compared to English falls today. But we have compensations; Dovedale, with its limestone shapes fantastically carved by water and weathered by wind, is one of them. And some of the human contributions, such as the great manmade lakes in the Elan Valley, where the waters of the Elan and Claerwen are held back by massive stone dams to supply the population of Birmingham, add a new dimension to the scene. This was one of the places where

Shelley thought of settling; he sailed paper boats in the Elan, but they sank and he went away.

Sometimes a river is the focal point of a landscape, sometimes it appears merely incidental, but always it is at work, eroding its bed and banks, transporting the material it has worn away, or that has been brought into it by rainfall or casual drainage, and depositing this material lower down, in a lake perhaps, or in its own lower reaches, or in the sea. Tidal action keeps estuaries from turning into deltas; even so, in many navigable rivers, constant dredging is necessary to maintain sufficient depth for sea-going craft. Over the centuries the Wash has been notorious for its shifting channels and training walls have had to be built for the rivers, Great Ouse, Nene, Welland and Witham, which find their outfalls there. Inland, oxbow lakes, some watered, some abandoned, show where meander loops were cut off as the river made for itself a new course many thousands of years ago. And it is still happening; the Coquet in Northumberland and the Cuckmere in Sussex are two rivers which are eating away at the curves in their courses.

In 1877 a list was compiled, for a Select Committee of the House of Lords, of all except the most minor rivers of England, Wales and Scotland. Tributaries were not listed by name, but their number and total length were included. We shall look at the eleven 'first-class' rivers, those with catchment basins of more than 1,000 square miles, later on, in their role as 'highways', but the other categories are more likely to include the favourite river of the individual than the first-class list which includes rivers known to all.

In the fifth class, with catchment basins of 10-50 square miles, there are 143 rivers, including the shortest of all—the Sillybrook in Glamorganshire, 2 miles long—and twenty-two anonymous streams. The twenty-four fourth-class rivers (covering 50-100 square miles) include Avon, Otter, Plym, Tavy and Taw in Devon, the Ehen, Ellen and Wampool—the name of this last, which meets the sea at Morecambe Bay, means 'a creek that may be waded at low tide', which seems somehow disappointing—in Cumberland, Northumberland Blyth and Suffolk Blythe, the Cuckmere and a handful of Welsh rivers. The Taw is the longest, but the Rhymney in South Wales has the largest catchment area.

In the third class, draining between 100 and 500 square miles, are fifty-eight rivers. The longest is the Wear, at 70 miles, and the shortest the Leven which, although less than 7 miles long, drains 123 square miles of Lancashire. In this group come the well known Sussex rivers, Arun, Adur, Ouse and Rother, the three famous Stours, of Dorset,

Kent and the Essex-Suffolk border, the Broadland Waveney and Bure, and some of the scenically most glorious rivers such as Dart, Tamar and Tweed. Many South Wales valley rivers come into this group, as well as the Conwy and the Dovey.

There are fourteen rivers in the second-class section (500-1,000 square miles). Here are the great Border rivers of Dee and Usk, the Tees, 95 miles long with nine major tributaries, the historic Medway, the Eden, largest river of the north west, the longest chalk streams in Hampshire, the Test and Avon, the Towy, longest river in South Wales, the Bristol Avon, Devonshire's Exe, the Ribble—as fine a river as any in the north of England—the Parrett, Welland and Yare. Comparable Scottish rivers are the Dee, Forth and Don. The first-class rivers are the great navigations of past and present, together with the Tay, Tweed, Clyde and Spey from north of the Border.

This list (printed in full in the Appendix) helps us to keep a sense of proportion and to see rivers as something more than elements in scenery. And the scenery itself is better seen than described in words. But often it has a meaning that needs to be made clear. We come back to the essential truth, that there can be no life without water. So, in some instances, it is possible to read the story of a river by standing back, as it were, and looking at it altogether. The Windrush is an example. Its name may be explained as 'white flowing'. It rises high in the Cotswolds and flows south easterly for about 30 miles to join the Thames at Newbridge, near Standlake. It is the second of the tributaries that come down to the Thames from the north between its source and Oxford, the others being the Coln, Churn, Leach, Evenlode and Cherwell.

The Windrush rises in a pool beside a road above the small village of Cutsdean, a rather bleak, tough-looking settlement, like a remote outpost of civilisation—which at a distant time it probably was. Here, reinforced by springs, it gathers strength and cuts a deeper valley. Soon it ducks under the B4077 road at Ford, the narrow bridge and the short, but steep, fall and rise adding to the perils of a notorious S-bend. From here it is easy to see, by walking or driving along the roads that keep the Windrush within sight—or even from the map—how the villages have grown up along the course of the river in this relatively unwatered countryside. There are the lovely cottages of Temple Guiting where the river runs between the church and the village itself. This is where the bishops of Oxford built their summer palace in the woodlands, the 'Temple' element in the name deriving from the Knights Templars who held estates hereabouts and owned fulling mills lower down the river at

The Windrush flowing through the centre of Bourton-on-the-Water, Gloucestershire

Barton. Before reaching Barton the Windrush runs through neat and tidy Kineton; below Barton a tributary stream comes in from the north west with Guiting Power on the valley side above it.

The river turns easterly to Naunton, a long village with a dovecote, a watermill and a reputation for healthiness in the late eighteenth century. After Harford Bridge, where the Cheltenham-Stow road crosses, there is a stretch of some 3 miles where river and a long abandoned railway line share the valley bottom. Meanwhile the landscape is changing, the hills fall back, the Roman Road, A429, crosses the river and here is Bourton-on-the-Water; first the mill, and then the main street with the river running along it, crossed by several arched footbridges, lined by grass and small trees. It has been a tourist centre for years and, like other small places similarly afflicted, it may seem to be a little self-conscious. Unlike others with similar opportunities, however, Bourton has turned its river to the best advantage, making it the focus of the settlement which, without it, might never have existed at all.

Below Bourton the valley broadens out; the Windrush is joined by the Dikler, which in turn has been augmented by the River Eye. On both these tributaries there are river-orientated villages; Upper and Lower Swell on the Dikler and Upper and Lower Slaughter on the Eye. The Windrush, now a sizeable stream, flows quietly southwards through fertile country, crossed by one bridge in 5 miles. The villages stand back, Great Rissington on the slopes to the east and Sherborne on its brook with its park, weirs and large gardens. The river swings east a few hundred yards from the village to which it has given its name, Windrush village with its mill and weir. Near the river now are the old quarries where stone was hewn for St Paul's: Barrington, Taynton and Burford. Wychwood Forest once came down to the northern bank of the river and Burford grew up on the southern side. With quarries, mills, tanneries and toll-bridge, Burford was a flourishing market town in the Middle Ages and many of its present buildings date from the fifteenth century. For a time its fortunes slumped; then for 150 years it became a horse-racing centre and an important halt on the London-Gloucester-South Wales coaching route. The railway ignored it, but the Society for the Preservation of Ancient Buildings was founded in consequence of William Morris's campaign against the restoration of Burford church. Now, like Bourton, it is a tourist attraction; when the tourist season begins, at Easter, it is worth recalling that it was at Burford where a council met in AD 683 to bring the date of that movable feast in England in line with that observed by the rest of the Church.

From Burford the Windrush continues in a deep valley; in the old hamlet of Widford there was a mill which, in turn, served as a fulling-mill, then a paper-mill and lastly a flour-mill. Akeman Street crosses the river; there is a blanket-mill near Worsham; and then the cottages, fine church and ruined manor of Minster Lovel. These buildings were constructed in the second part of the fifteenth century. Francis Lovel became a supporter of Richard III and gained immortality through Shakespeare as 'Lovel the Dog'. After Bosworth he escaped to France, later to support the absurd claim of Lambert Simnel to the throne. Legend tells that, after defeat, he returned to hide in the family home. In 1708, when a new chimney was being built, an underground vault was discovered 'in which there was the entire skeleton of a man, as having been sitting at a table, which was before him, with a book, paper, pen etc'. Also in the room was the skeleton of a dog, and a cap

23

'much mouldered and decayed'. This, it is assumed, was Francis, who had died of starvation.

It is difficult to describe a river without continually wandering away from it. Minster Lovel is the most romantic of the Windrush settlements and the next one, Witney, the largest and most businesslike. The Domesday Book records two mills at Witney; for centuries it has been a weaving town, specialising in blankets for over 300 years. A particular chemical content of Windrush water makes it so valuable in the soaking and whitening processes, and the prosperity of the blanket makers is reflected in the extent of the town, the quality of its buildings and the size of its church.

Below Witney the river divides naturally into two arms with the site of an occasional mill and the substance of a weir on each. They rejoin below Broad Bridges; soon there is a wide weir, Newbridge Mill, the lowest bridge. As it approaches the Thames, the Windrush seems to shrink; undramatically the waters merge above Newbridge and the lovely old Rose Revived.

As one can see in the topmost reaches of a river a whole river system in miniature, so in a small river, such as the Windrush, can we see the miniaturisation of a larger one. It is more fun to make the comparison yourself; Windrush and Thames, for example, or Teme and Severn, or Monnow and Wye. The similarities are in the pattern, the differences in the detail. An old edition of the Ordnance Survey map is a useful aid as it will show more watermill sites and will help to explain the positioning of weirs and the complicated pattern of small channels that served as leats or tail-races. Despite Viscount Torrington's rather tetchy attitude—'When was any river made navigable that its beauties were not demolished?' he asked—evidence of navigation, past or present, often adds to a river's attractiveness and interest. The Lee, scenically rather a dull river, is brought to life by boats, and the riverside buildings at Ware remind us of the Lee's past trading history. The locks, bridges and riverside pubs on the Soar Navigation—at Mountsorrel, for instance, or Barrow—increase the interest of this somewhat ordinary river. Exploration of the Sussex Ouse, the Ivel in Bedfordshire, the Wreak in Leicestershire reveals the remains of locks and other navigation works, and excites the imagination.

The Wey is a good example of an easily accessible river which has, as it were, worked hard for its living and gives a great deal of pleasure to those who use it today. From many sources in the Hampshire and Surrey hills a number of streams flow and merge, eventually to unite at Tilford. The Wey flows through Godalming, pierces the chalk hills at Guildford and meets the Thames below Shepperton lock. In its time the main river, with its various tributaries and branches, has powered some fifty mills, of which the great weatherboarded Newark Mill, by the ruins of Newark Priory near Ripley, is a handsome survivor on a site where a mill has been for over 700 years. In 1653 the Wey was made navigable to Guildford, with twelve locks and several lengths of new channel, and it was extended to Godalming just over a century later. In 1794 a 37½ mile canal was opened from the river near Byfleet to Basingstoke, and in 1816 the Wey & Arun Canal linked the Surrey and Sussex rivers. This navigation was extended to Portsmouth a few years later, forming a direct water route from London to the coast.

The Wey was a profitable navigation. In its earlier years great quantities of timber were carried to London, much of it being floated down on the current, guided by a man with a pole. 'This navigation is also a mighty support to the great corn-market at Farnham,' said Defoe; indeed, the grain traffic continued on the river as far as Guildford until 1950 and the last boat from London docks to Coxes Mill above Weybridge sailed in 1969. For over a hundred years the Stevens family controlled the river up to Guildford. Mr H. W. Stevens handed the river over to the National Trust in 1964, and the Commissioners of the Godalming Navigation (the river between Guildford and Godalming) did likewise four years later. In the Trust's own words: 'It will be maintained permanently as a waterway for boats, fishermen and for those who like to walk, or paint on the towpath.' By the river there are handsome houses—Sutton Place is probably the best known—attractive villages, good pubs and ancient churches. Except in the lower reaches, it flows through varied and beautiful countryside, not dramatic or in any way spectacular, but small scale and friendly. It is a good river to take a boat on in winter.

If you were to stand by the source of the westernmost headwater of the Wey and walk due east across the heart of the Weald as far as the Eastern Stour in Kent, you would have to cross more than twenty-five streams and rivers. North, to the Thames, flow the Wey, Mole and Darent and their tributaries; eastward flow Eden and Medway, joined by Teise, Beult and other streams. Southward, towards the Channel, run the Western Rother, Arun, Adur, Ouse and Cuckmere. The pattern is not altogether a simple one; the streams take the easiest courses through the more permeable rock until it is as if they gather together into rivers to force their way through the chalk barriers of the north and South Downs. But if, starting from the same headwater of the Wey, you were to walk a similar distance due west, you would cross fewer than ten rivers or streams, the Itchen and Test, rising in the Hampshire Downs, and the tributaries of the Salisbury Avon. The Weald, indeed, is one of the areas most prolific in water, rivalled only by central Devon and parts of the mountainous country of Wales, the Pennines and the Highlands. The phenomenon that geologists call 'river capture' is also happening in the Weald, where the Arun is taking over the supplies of the Adur and the Blackwater is yielding to the Wey. Another clear example of this phenomenon can be seen in Northumberland, where the Tyne has taken over the headstreams of the Hart Burn, the Wansbeck and the Blyth. It has, indeed, 'beheaded' them.

Rivers, for the most part, unify a landscape rather than divide it. Having carved their valleys and created their flood plains, formed their waterfalls, terraces and levees, they become for each generation part of a favourite scene at a particular moment in time. The great rivers of history—Thames, Severn, Dee and Forth—the rivers of 'swirling pools, gliding shallows, the angry rock-fretted rapids, mossy crags and fringing woods'—Usk, Wye, Tyne, Dove, Dart—the three Avons of Bristol, Warwickshire and Hampshire, the rivers of the Yorkshire Dales, the Ribble and Hodder of Lancashire, the fierce Highland streams and the slow, winding, water highways of the east of England—Witham, Nene, Great Ouse, Waveney, Bure and Yare—each has its place in the countryman's heart, each has its interest, its pleasure, its delight.

2

WORKING RIVERS

At Trumpington, nat fer fro Cantebrigge,
Ther goth a brook and over that a brigge,
Upon the whiche brook ther stant a melle;

So Oswald the Reeve began his story in *The Canterbury Tales*. In
Chaucer's time the watermill was an essential part of the fabric of life
and the miller was as indispensable as the grocer is today to the village or
the supermarket to the town. Traditionally he was an unpopular figure;
the miller of Oswald's tale had a monopoly of the local trade, grinding
the wheat and malt 'of al the land aboute' and notorious for stealing
much of what passed through his mill. We look back at this sturdy, hot-
tempered, dishonest fellow across the centuries and do not altogether
regret his passing.

But what of the watermill? A few years ago it seemed in danger of
disappearing entirely, except for a few conversions into private homes or
restaurants. Then to the rescue came the industrial archaeologists, just
in time to save, for example, Preston Mill on the River Tyne in East
Lothian, now restored and back in operation as a working watermill.
Preston Mill, with its kiln, dates from the seventeenth century, an
exceptional age for mill buildings which normally were unable to
withstand the constant vibration for much more than 200 years. While
the sites on which they stand may date back to Domesday Book or
before, most of the mills themselves were rebuilt time and time again.

Preston was one of a succession of mills along its river, originally built
when water was the primary—and in some places the only—source of
power. All the earliest mills—and it is most likely that the Romans
introduced them to Britain, Chesters on the North Tyne, Willowford on
the Irthing and Haltcastle Burn Head being among the probable sites—

Preston Mill, East Linton, by the River Tyne in East Lothian. The weathervane on the top of the kiln is known as 'the long arm of friendship'

were built to grind corn. By the time of the Domesday survey there was a total of 5,624 watermills recorded in England, omitting the northern counties. Top of the list came Norfolk with 301 and next was Lincolnshire with 256. Tennyson was born at Somersby, on the River Steeping; in his poem 'The Miller's Daughter' he wrote about Stockworth Mill nearby:

> I loved the brimming wave that swam
> Thro' quiet meadows round the mill,
> The sleepy pool above the dam,
> The pool beneath it never still,
> The meal-sacks on the whiten'd floor,
> The dark round of the dripping wheel . . .

The 'dripping wheel' at Stockworth today is the same one that Tennyson saw, remade in the eighteenth century with an iron rim and castings affixed by wooden spokes to the older wooden axle. There is another old Lincolnshire mill at Alvingham near Louth, on the little River Lud; here the machinery still works and the buildings are open to the public at various times in the summer months.

For a mill to be built in the first place, there had to be a community to be fed, a supply of locally grown corn, a willing landowner with an eye to profit, as the mills originally belonged to the owners of the land on which they were built, and of course a sufficient flow of water. It is thought that a Domesday mill served the needs of about fifty households, and it was not until a century after the survey that windmills were introduced to supplement, and in some instances to replace, those powered by water. One of the oldest recorded sites is at Houghton on the Great Ouse, between St Ives and Huntingdon; here a mill has stood since the year 969 at least and corn was being ground in the present building, itself about 200 years old, until well into the twentieth century. Houghton was one of twenty-three Domesday mills in the county of Huntingdonshire, all powered by the Great Ouse or its tributaries. Even little Rutland had twenty-one mills, three more than those listed for the whole county of Cheshire.

Another survivor on one of the earliest sites is the handsome white weatherboarded mill at Hambledon on a backwater of the Thames. Here the rent, including the right to take 1,000 eels from the river, was £1 a year in 1086. But the cost of building a mill at Acton Round on the Rea Brook in Shropshire, over 200 years later, was only £6 18s 7d (£6.93), and this included the digging of a pond and ditch. The two millstones themselves cost 24s (£1.20); against these figures the Hambledon rental falls into perspective. As payment for his services, a medieval miller was entitled to one-sixteenth of the flour he ground—a system clearly open to abuse. In the fourteenth and fifteenth centuries, however, it became more usual for a miller to own his mill, and his social status rose in consequence. No longer were tenants of a particular manor compelled to send their corn to the manor's own mill and gradually the miller's unpopularity and reputation for dishonesty faded away.

The primary use of the watermill was the grinding of corn, but the principle was easily adapted for other purposes. With the development of weaving came the introduction, in the second half of the twelfth century, of the fulling-mill in which cloth, soaked in water, was beaten with trip-hammers powered by the waterwheel. This improved the

Sluices at Jordan's Mill on the Ivel, Bedfordshire

density of the cloth as well as pre-shrinking it. In Wales and Cornwall fulling-mills were known as pandy- and tucking-mills respectively; Tonypandy in the Rhondda is 'the untilled land where the fulling-mills are'. Next came tanning-mills, crushing tan bark or woad to make dye. Later, watermills were adapted for papermaking, gunpowder-grinding—Chart Mill at Faversham in Kent is the oldest of these—preparing leather, tobacco and snuff, flint-grinding—Cheddleton flint-mills on the Churnet, restored to working order in 1969 and open to public view, ground flint for use in the potteries nearby—for boring guns and cylinders and for sawing timber. The Tillingbourne in Surrey, a tributary of the Wey, drove eight mills in its 10-mile course, for corn, weaving, tanning, gunpowder and the iron industry. Chilworth was the gunpowder centre and the tanneries were concentrated at Gomshall. There were corn- and hammer-mills at Shere, and the name of the village of Abinger Hammer derives from the sixteenth-century forge that was powered by the Tillingbourne. The hammer-ponds, dug to provide extra water, are now watercress beds. The River Sheaf provided the power for the early steel works at Sheffield, and you can visit a restored water-powered scythe and steel works at the Abbeydale Industrial Hamlet, 3½ miles south west of the city centre. The wool industry of Gloucestershire grew up in the valleys of the Frome and Avon, while in Hertfordshire papermaking became an important local industry alongside the Ver, Lee, Chess, Colne and Bulbourne. Sopwell Mill on the Ver began as a corn-mill, was converted to papermaking and reverted to corn-grinding all in the seventeenth century. The method of making paper in rolls instead of single sheets was imported from France by Henry Fourdrinier who had two mills on the Gade; John Dickinson of Apsley Mill on the same river followed his example and expanded his business to take in three more mills, later converted to steam power. Apsley and Croxley are familiar names in writing paper today. There were, indeed, about 400 paper-mills at work in the early nineteenth century, not all of them in Hertfordshire; the largest of them was Peckwash on the Derbyshire Derwent, which at one time had five waterwheels driving four papermaking machines and remained in operation until 1906.

The River Wandle, 9 miles long from South Croydon to the Thames at Wandsworth, was described in 1805 as 'the hardest worked river for its size in the world'. A fast-flowing river, it provided ideal conditions for mill working. Domesday lists thirteen Wandle mills; by 1600 there were twenty-four. In 1831 there were ninety, but by that date the water level was falling and soon the steam engine was to drive the watermills out of trade. The Wandle mills in their time ground corn, dyewoods, gunpowder, hemp and drugs; they made paper, processed leather and oil, powered copper and iron works, printed silk, made felt, fulled cloth and distilled peppermint and lavender. Liberty's of Regent Street owned a print-mill at Merton. The river had its own calico industry, with its water being used to bleach the cloth dried along its banks. Watercress grew in the river—you may still be able to find some at Carshalton—and, until the mid-nineteenth century, it was famous as a trout stream. Thereafter both the trout and the water-powered industries rapidly declined; by 1889 the river was 'littered with the corpses of dead industries', water was being abstracted from the upper reaches to supply the needs of South London, and what was left was becoming foul. Much of the river has been diverted or culverted and much effluent is still discharged into it; some hope for the preservation and improvement of the river lies in the local conservation societies and the concern of the local authorities, whose efforts to 'secure the future well-being' of the river are co-ordinated by the Wandle Group.

The Wandle mills served a wide area. In the north east of England, however, the mills in general catered only for the needs of the immediate locality. They were small buildings, seldom more than two stories high, grinding a few sacks of grain at a time. In the uplands it was often impossible to build the mills close to the streams; hence the water often had to be carried to the wheel in long wooden troughs. One of the most famous is the tweed-mill at Otterburn in Northumberland, converted to the processing of wool in 1821. It is now driven by electricity and not by the waters of the Otterburn itself. Another well known millstream was the Ouseburn, a tributary of the Tyne which it joins in Newcastle. This powered several corn- and flint-mills; the remains of two of them still survive in the park of Jesmond Dene.

During a recent survey of watermills in the old East Riding of Yorkshire, the sites of all those recorded as working in 1850 were visited. Very few were situated on main rivers; there were only three on the Derwent and one on the Ouse. Most of them were on small streams, sometimes merely called 'Mill Beck' or named after a local village, and in all of them the wheel was positioned inside the building. All those operating in 1850—except for the snuff-mill at Cottingham—were grinding corn. Of the total of fifty-nine, three were still at work, modernised and electrically operated, and twenty-one had been demolished. The remainder had all been converted to different uses, including storage, piggeries, garages and dwellings, while the big mill at Stamford Bridge, which once had two wheels and seven pairs of stones, is now a hotel and restaurant.

Water power for milling was best provided by the natural fall of the river or stream. The River Kent in Westmorland, falling 1,000ft in about 25 miles, has probably the fastest flow in England and drove the many mills of the woollen trade which grew up in and around Kendal in the fourteenth century—Falstaff's lie about the 'knaves in Kendal Green' recalls the local cloth. Where the flow was insufficient, weirs were constructed to build up a head of water. An undershot wheel, turned by water striking it below the axle, was the simplest to install. Water was led to the wheel via a mill-race and returned to the main stream along a tail-race. More efficient was the overshot wheel, but it needed a greater velocity of water to turn it. Breast wheels, struck by the water about axle level, and pitch-back wheels—overshot wheels working

(*opposite*) An early-eighteenth-century plan of the Nene, before the navigation works began

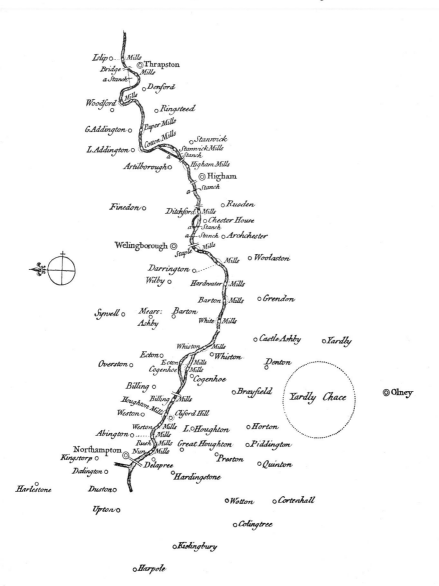

A PLAN *of the* RIVER NEN, *from* Thrapston *to* Northampton *with the* Mills and Locks *necessary for the Navigation, together with the Towns near the River.*

The Dotted Lines shew on which side of the River the Locks are to be fixed.

Islip ○ ... ◖Mills
Bridge ○ ◎ Thrapston
a Stanch Mills
○ Denford
Woodford Mills
○ ○ Ringsteed
G.Addington ○ Paper Mills
Cotton Mills
L.Addington ○ ○ Stanwick
a ◖ Stanwick Mills
Artilborough ○ ◖ Stanch
◖ Higham Mills
◎ Higham
a ◖ Stanch
Finedon ○ ○ Rusden
Ditchford ◖ Mills
○ Chester House
a ◖ Stanch
a ◖ Stanch ○ Archchester
Welingborough ◎ ◖ Mills
Staple
Darrington ○ ... ◖ Mills ○ Woolaston
Wilby ○ Hardwater ◖ Mills
Barton ◖ Mills ○ Grendon
Synvell ○ Mears: Barton ○
Ashby White ◖ Mills
Whiston ◖ Mills ○ Castle Ashby ○ Yardly
Ecton ○ Ecton ◖ Mills ○ Whiston
Overston ○ Cogenhoe ◖ Mills ○ Denton
○ Cogenhoe
Billing ○ ○ Braysfield Yardly Chace ◎ Olney
Houghton Mills Billing ◖ Mills
Weston ○ ○ Clsford Hill
Weston ◖ Mills L. ○ Houghton ○ Horton
Abington ○ ... ◖ Mills
Northampton Rush ◖ Mills Great Houghton ○ Piddington
Kingstorp ○ Nun ◖ Mills ○ Preston ○ Quinton
Dalington ○ ○ Delapree ○ Hardingstone
Harlestone ○ Duston ○
Upton ○ ○ Wotton ○ Cortenhall
○ Colingtree
○ Kislingbury
○ Harpole

33

in the reverse direction—were other variations chosen to suit particular circumstances. Weirs, hatches, sluices, eel-traps, pits, subterranean and bypass channels, races and leats—all are components of the watermill scene. Each mill has its own characteristic arrangement, and has left its own individual signature on the landscape. But, until John Smeaton published his *Inquiry into the Powers of Wind and Water*, the technology was mostly by rule of thumb. With iron now available for the wheels, Smeaton himself designed several watermills, the first in 1753 at Halton, near Lancaster. Among his major achievements was the large waterwheel for the London Bridge waterworks, installed 1767-8.

On the navigable rivers, millers and boatmen were often in contention. For a working river to be made navigable, it was usually necessary for locks to be constructed so that boats could pass the weirs. On the Nene, for example, there were twenty-one mills between Northampton and Thrapston, and a lock was built by each one. The by-laws imposed penalties on the millers for holding up or letting down water without giving boat-owners stipulated notice, but the records are peppered with complaints against the millers for impeding the navigation by drawing off water. Some of the Nene mills still remain; Billing Mill, near Northampton, has been restored as a museum of milling and can be seen in action, while the mill at Oundle has been converted into a restaurant. Mills are still operating by two of the oldest

Letheringham Watermill on the Deben in Suffolk

sites, at Wellingborough and at Bugbrooke, above the head of navigation at Northampton, where the present vast complex is on the site of two mills mentioned in Domesday.

While some of the nineteenth-century brick-built mills have more appeal to industrial archaeologists than to lovers of the picturesque, the eighteenth-century—and older—buildings generally show a characteristic blend of useful purpose and architectural harmony. Letheringham Mill, on the Deben, built on a Domesday site with a Tudor house and the mill itself dating from about 1720, is a fine example, set in beautiful grounds open to the public. Most watermills seem to have enjoyed an uneventful history, but at Letheringham there was a murder most foul in 1696 when Jonah Snell, a servant, seized an axe and killed John Bullard, the miller, and his son. Snell was hanged; the remains of the gibbet may still be found in nearby Potsford Wood. Letheringham stopped working early this century, when its machinery was removed to the windmill at Kelsale. Still at work, however, are the Deben Mills at Wickham Market close by.

Other water-powered mills include Rowsley Mill on the Derbyshire Wye—now operated by turbines instead of a wheel—and two mills on the Dorset Stour, Sturminster and Fiddleford. The machinery at Sturminster is comparatively modern, but Fiddleford has two pairs of Derbyshire stones driven by water. A few months ago this stretch of the Stour was in peril; the level is controlled by a weir and a set of hatches which were being undermined and the banks eroded. Funds for improvement and repair work were quickly raised, a healthy sign of the interest and concern that people now have for watermills and their surroundings. Fiddleford will never attract the crowds that flock to England's best-known mills—Flatford and Dedham on the Suffolk Stour—but it is as fascinating in its own way—more so, perhaps, as it still fulfils its original purpose.

On the Deben estuary stands the last working example of the tide-mill. In the mid-1930s there were twenty-three of these at work; Woodbridge is the only survivor. Tide-mills were built on shallow creeks or estuaries—the lowest mill on the Wandle was a tide-mill—and required the digging of a large pond which was filled by the incoming tide. The pond at Woodbridge covered 7½ acres, small in comparison to the 30-acre pond at St Osyth's. As the tide flowed into the estuary it pushed open sluice gates and forced its way into the pond. The gates were closed by the pressure of the water behind them as the tide turned. The miller would then open sluice gates at the head of the mill-race, releasing the pent-up water which turned the millwheel on its way out.

Woodbridge Tide Mill, now restored and open to visitors

The wheel could operate for about two hours either side of low tide and the working of the mill depended on the tide-tables and seasonal variations. A tide-mill at Woodbridge was first recorded in 1170. The present structure dates from 1793; it laboured on, becoming progressively more dilapidated, until the wheel shaft broke in 1957. After some years of debate about its future—during which the large mill at St Osyth's was demolished—the Woodbridge Mill was bought by Mrs R. T. Gardner and handed over to a specially formed trust. Public appeals raised enough money to begin restoration, estimated to cost in all nearly £100,000. By 1977 the machinery had been restored and the whole building opened to the public, with displays of photographs and milling equipment.

Much of Britain's industrial and commercial prosperity derived from the waterwheel. Power for industries in towns as different as Winchester and Manchester was provided by rivers as different as the Itchen and the Irk. The fulling-mills of the Irk, incidentally, provided more than power. 'I have eaten eels out of 30 rivers,' wrote James Chetham in *The Angler's Vade Mecum* in 1681, 'yet none that I ever met with were to be compared for goodness and deliciousness of taste to the eels caught in a small river in Lancashire called the Irk . . . and having often enquired of

36

the neighbouring People to it what might be the reason, they have unanimously ascribed it to the numerousness of Fulling Mills that stand on that River, and say that the Fat, Oil and Grease scoured out of the Cloth, makes the Eels palatable and far above other River Eels.' Modern industrial use of rivers is not always so beneficial to fish. But the emphasis has now shifted from the natural sources of power to the generation of electricity, and rivers have been put to work in a different way that has made spectacular and sometimes controversial changes to the landscape.

The reason for the siting of power stations on rivers is simple. No matter what fuel the station consumes, an adequate supply of cooling water is essential. To produce one unit of electricity, a bathful of water has to pass through a power station's condensers, and the Central Electricity Generating Board produces about 200,000 million units a year. To cope with this would soon exhaust the river system. Hence the cooling towers, which dominate many river reaches; these towers enable the same water to be used over and over again, with only a 1 per cent loss in vapour, which the river itself can easily supply. The only power stations that do not recirculate their cooling water are some of the older and smaller ones and those situated on the coast.

For two main reasons—the proximity of the East Midlands coalfield and the quantity of cooling water available—the Trent valley has now the largest concentration of power stations in the country. There are twelve major installations: Meaford, Rugeley, Drakelow, Willington, Castle Donington, Ratcliffe-on-Soar, Wilford, Staythorpe, High Marnham, Cottam, West Burton and Keadby. There are four more stations on Trent tributaries, three of them on the Tame and one on the Derwent. The CEGB has to ensure that the water returned to the river after use is not so hot that it would cook the fish; indeed, it is claimed that the warmed water encourages fish development, and experiments in fish-farming are being carried out at Ironbridge power station on the Severn.

The power stations of the Trent and other English rivers are hardly tourist attractions; for many people, enjoyment of their visual aspect is probably an acquired taste. But the hydro-electric power stations of the north of Scotland are in a different class; the North of Scotland Hydro-Electric Board says that over 100,000 tourists visit its installations and exhibition at Pitlochry every year, and a further 50,000 go to Cruachan to see the underground power station there. With hydro-elecricity, generators are driven by water turbines, the water being drawn from the rivers and lochs of the Highlands. There are four main groups of

High Marnham Power Station on the flooded Trent, 1977

stations, supplying about 40 per cent of the requirements of the area, the rest being met by a large oil-powered station at Dundee and by transference from southern Scotland. The Board itself came into being in 1943 and since then has built more than fifty dams and hydro stations.

One of the four groups is Tummel-Breadalbane, in the centre of the Board's area. The River Tummel is the principal tributary of the Tay; with its own tributaries, the Tummel's waters produce about 640 million units of electricity a year out of the total annual hydro-electric output of 2,945 million units. Eight stations are served by the Tummel, its tributaries and lochs; in the interests of the salmon, fish-passes have been made at Pitlochry Dam, Clunie Dam, Dunalastair Dam, Kinloch Rannoch weir and Gaur, where a pass of seventy pools enables the salmon to reach Loch Eigheach to spawn. The Pitlochry pass is typical of the earlier fish-passes; it is over 1,000ft long and contains thirty-four pools connected by underwater pipes, with a rise of 18in between each. The newer type of pass—the Borland fish-pass—works like a pound lock, demanding no effort on the part of the fish and economising on water. There are now seventeen Borland passes in operation.

Other Highland rivers whose waters have been harnessed in this way include the Conon and its tributaries, the Beauly, Affric, Fyne and Moriston, and a number of smaller rivers and streams in the far north. The Board's architects and engineers have successfully integrated their installations into the landscape, with tact in the selection of materials used and an impressive boldness in design.

So far we have looked at rivers as sources, direct or contributory, of power. Water is an industry in its own right, and the supply of water for domestic and industrial use is a major function of our rivers. From the Severn nearly 170 million gallons a day are abstracted, and the Clywedog reservoir was constructed in 1968 to maintain the flow in dry weather. The river's tributaries affect the quality of the Severn water. The tributaries of the upper river and the Teme, which joins the Severn below Worcester, bring in good quality water at the head of the reach which supplies Coventry, Cheltenham and Gloucester. But the Worcestershire Stour is heavily polluted as it passes through the industrial area west of Birmingham and affects the quality of the main river for some miles below Stourport. The Avon suffers from the injection of sewage and, except above Rugby, is unsuitable for public water supply. At the Tewkesbury confluence, however, the flow of the Severn is about five times that of the Avon and the effect of the polluted water is only minor.

The waters of the Trent are affected to an even greater extent by its tributaries. The main river itself deteriorates below Stoke-on-Trent but is revived by the good water from the River Sow at Great Haywood. Next comes the Tame, notoriously dirty, downgrading the Trent's quality for over 90 miles. Both Dove and Derwent are clean, especially the former; the Soar is not too bad, the Erewash is polluted, the Leen is good quality, but the Devon and Idle carry sewage and industrial waste and significant quantities of saline mine water.

The Yorkshire Derwent illustrates how an area depends on a clean river for its water supply. This river, 75 miles long from its source to the junction with the Ouse, serves one-seventh of the population of Yorkshire. Water is taken off through a treatment works at Elvington to a point west of Selby. The pipeline then divides, to supply Leeds to the west and Sheffield to the south. To increase supplies from the Derwent a tidal barrage has been constructed at Barmby which enables a further 55,000 cubic metres to be taken off every day via pipeline to Kingston-upon-Hull. Some idea of the problems water engineers have to face can

Pitlochry Dam and Fish Pass

be gained from looking at the figures of the rate of flow of the Derwent, taken at the gauging station above Elvington. The average flow of the river is 17 cubic metres a second, but this can increase to about 170 cubic metres in flood conditions and can fall to as little as 3 cubic metres in the driest weather.

In 1976 Yorkshire—or to be exact the Yorkshire Water Authority—drew 20 per cent of its total water supply from rivers. The figures for the other water authorities show rivers generally providing between 18 and 32 per cent of the supply. But there are remarkable variations; in the Wessex area, for instance, while Bristol draws half its supply from rivers, the rest of the region relies entirely on reservoirs and groundwater. In the Anglian region groundwater makes the largest contribution—74 per cent—and in Cornwall the smallest, only 5 per cent. Natural lakes, as a glance at the map will quickly show, contribute only in the northern part of England.

In the history of the water industry there are two great monuments. The first is a river made for the sole purpose of water supply—the New river, cut between 1608 and 1613 on the orders of Alderman Hugh

Myddleton, to convey water from Chadwell and Great Amwell springs, south of Ware in Hertfordshire, to London. It was an ambitious and expensive undertaking, and to complete it Myddleton had to accept help from James I. In 1619 he formed the New River Company, which eventually became enormously profitable and lasted until it was taken over by the Metropolitan Water Board in 1904. The New river, between 15 and 20ft wide, flows down the Lee valley to a reservoir at New River Head, Clerkenwell. Thence the water used to be conveyed by wooden pipes around the city. When the springs proved unable to meet the demand, an Act of Parliament was obtained in 1738 enabling a cut to be made from the Lee to the New river and a gauge to measure the amount of water transferred was installed. The 1856 model of this gauge is still in use, showing the average daily inflow from the Lee to be about 22½ million gallons.

The second monument is the Kew Bridge Pumping Station whose engines, which operated until 1944, are now being restored. There are five engines at Kew Bridge, the earliest, a Boulton & Watt, made in 1820. Both this and a 90in Cornish beam engine dating from 1845 are back in working order as a result of the efforts of the Kew Bridge Engine Trust whose intention is to restore all the engines including the massive 100in Cornish monster installed in 1869. The site is open to the public at weekends. The Kew station pumped Thames water into the West London mains; it has been said that when the 1869 engine joined the others 'there was probably more man-made power concentrated at Kew than anywhere else in the world'. Mention of Boulton & Watt recalls the one engine made by that firm which still performs its original function. This is the pumping engine at Crofton, feeding the Kennet & Avon Canal from Wilton Water, 40ft below. It was installed in 1812 and worked until 1958; since then, the Kennet & Avon Trust has restored it to full working order. Crofton can be seen in steam on various weekends and is the oldest working steam engine in existence.

In the history of water supply there ought also to be a place for Susan Cuckson and Dolly Hurst. In times long past, these ladies supplied water to the town of Gainsborough, Susan with two buckets on a yoke and Dolly with a water cart which she filled at a landing place on the Trent, selling the water at a halfpenny a bucket in the lower part of the town and a penny if she had to carry it up the hill. The efforts of Susan and Dolly were supplemented by Simon Patricke's pump in the Market Place; in 1635 he was being paid five shillings a year to keep it in good order. By 1795 Gainsborough had a waterworks: three small pumps operated by a horse and, when the tide was in, filling a cistern some ten

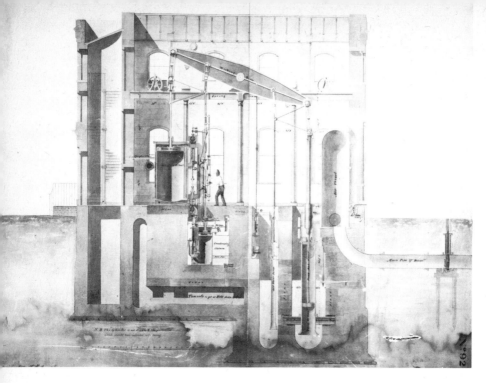

(*above*) The Boulton & Watt engine as erected at Chelsea before being moved to Kew Bridge; (*below*) 100in engine beam at Kew Bridge

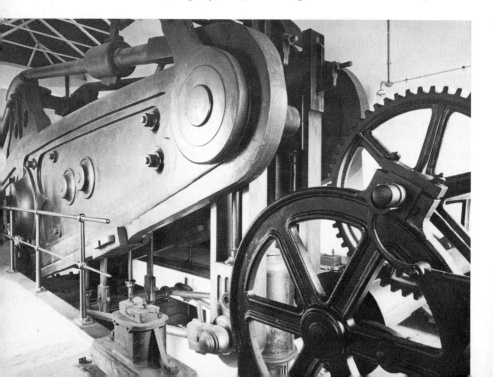

feet above ground which fed the water through pipes to the main streets of the town. Taps, each of which served several houses, were placed at intervals along the pipes. William Crabtree, who owned the waterworks in 1844, charged his consumers £1 a year. The waterworks were enlarged and eventually taken over by the local Board of Health in 1871. Until 1890 the supply continued to come from the river, but since then three boreholes have been sunk and the town's water is raised through these.

After all that, what about a pause for refreshment? To Scotland then, and to the River Spey. There are about a hundred pot-still malt-whisky distilleries in Scotland, and every distiller is jealous of his water supply. The malts of Skye and Islay have their devotees, but the Speyside malts are the most popular and most widely distributed. Glenlivet is perhaps the best known name in Scotch whisky; the River Livet is a tributary of the Avon, which is itself a tributary of the Spey. George Smith obtained a licence for the first legal distillery in Glenlivet in 1824, a year after the Act providing for annual licensing and duty was passed. But for years before then the illicit whisky distilled by Smith at Drumin, near the confluence of Livet and Avon, had the reputation of being the finest in the Highlands; George IV enjoyed it when he visited Scotland in 1822. Other well known distilleries include Glen Grant at Rothes, near the junction of the Burn of Rothes and the Spey, and Glenfiddich on the River Fiddich, another Spey tributary. But the primacy of Glenlivet is attested by the fact that no fewer than eighteen distilleries incorporate it in their brand-names. Many of the Speyside distilleries are open to the public and, consequently, this has become a tourist area. As long as the water remains undefiled the quality of the Scottish malts will persist.

For distillers, then, purity of their water is essential. Elsewhere for centuries rivers and streams have been used as channels for the disposal of waste of all kinds. Until the industrial development of the nineteenth century the rivers, for the most part, could cope with the task; both salmon and oysters used to be found in the Thames, for example. With the rapid growth of both industry and population all this changed. By the early 1800s the rivers of industrial Lancashire were devoid of all life; birds could walk across the black and stinking Irwell. Charles Dickens in his novels and periodicals returned time and again to the subject of polluted rivers, the Thames especially. He was editor of *Household Words* and in July 1858 published the following:

> When our middle-aged people were young, cesspools were a national institution. Filth soaked into the ground under our houses, or was dug thence periodically, and disposed of by hand-labour for economic

purposes; baths were in less general use; a modest water supply was enough for any town, and it carried away with it through the sewers into the rivers no very large quantity of offensive refuse. But, since we have discovered the great danger of dirt, and have ceased to pollute the soil on which we build our houses, we have established a new system which is not yet complete in all its parts. With a full water supply we seek to wash out of any decent town the whole mass of the filth generated in it . . . We pour it out into the rivers flowing through our towns, and pollute them as never before have rivers been polluted since the world was made. The soot-coloured river at Manchester; the Tame at Birmingham, a small stream which, even before reaching Birmingham, receives much of the animal refuse of two hundred and seventy thousand persons; may be said in a dry season to contain as much sewage as water. The Thames which, before reaching London, is polluted by the drainage from seven hundred thousand people, and in London deposits the filth of hundreds of thousands upon mudbanks exposed daily at low water, and in these hot days festering at the heart of the metropolis.

The situation in London had been unwittingly made worse by the Metropolitan Commissioners of Sewers, who had abolished the individual cesspools in the poorer districts and attached the dwellings to main sewers discharging directly into the river. But in the same year as this article appeared Sir Joseph Bazalgette, engineer to the newly created Metropolitan Board of Works, obtained parliamentary approval for his scheme. In the following years two large main sewers were constructed, one on each side of the Thames, leading to outfalls at Barking and Crossness. It was some years later when the outfall effluents began to be treated—uncomfortable times for those living nearby. You can still find some of the pumping houses built by the Board of Works as part of this scheme.

This was the first step towards a solution of the problems of disposing of London's waste. It needed the combined efforts of scientists and engineers for over a century before the tidal Thames could again be described as 'living'—the story is told in two books published in 1977, *The Living Thames* and *The Thames Transformed*, the latter describing in detail the return of wildlife to the tidal river. But no one can yet write a book called *The Living Tame*, and it is sad that in 1977 the condition of such a beautiful river as the Cam has deteriorated to the point when it is no longer safe to swim in its waters.

The last of the main functions of the working river is land drainage—although perhaps it would be better to regard it as the first. God was the first of the drainers, as Sir William Dugdale pointed out in the first

chapter of his *History of Imbanking and Draining*, 1662: 'That works of Draining are most antient, and of divine institution, we have the testimony of holy Scripture: "In the beginning God said, 'Let the waters be gathered together, and let the dry land appear'; and it was so; And the earth brought forth grass, and herb yielding seed, and the fruit-tree yielding fruit after his kind; and God saw that it was good."'
Dugdale describes undertakings in the Near East, Southern Europe, Holland and America, and in several English counties before turning to the Great Level of the Fens, the chief subject of his work. Nowadays drainage refers to the seasonal running-off of surplus water, but in earlier years it meant the reclamation of lost or drowned lands. The Romans were the pioneers of English drainage, cutting many waterways for the dual purposes of drainage and navigation including the Fossdyke in Lincolnshire, the Car Dyke from the Cam at Waterbeach to the Fossdyke near Lincoln, and some of the Cambridgeshire lodes. After the Romans, however, there was for centuries no organised direction or administration of drainage works; whatever was done—and that was not very much—was done by individual effort.

In the mid-thirteenth century the first commissions of sewers were set up to deal with the problem at local level. The commissioners for an area enquired into the problem by holding inquisitions; where trouble occurred they made a survey and ordered a remedy. Landowners might be instructed to repair the banks of a stream, or a local tax could be levied to raise money for scouring out ditches. Later the commissioners were empowered to summon juries which gave them the authority to act without having to go to law. But the function of commissions of sewers was limited to repair; generally they could only order the patching up of what was already there and they did not initiate new works.

Perhaps the greatest single drainage undertaking between Roman times and the seventeenth century was the 12-mile cut still known as Morton's Leam. This was made at the order of Bishop Morton of Ely during the 1470s. The leam was 40ft wide and 4ft deep, taking the water of the Nene in an almost straight line from just below Peterborough to Guyhirne, for both drainage and navigation. The bishop built a tower at Guyhirne from which he could oversee the works. The leam was enlarged in 1570 and further improved early in the seventeenth century. It was, in fact, the main channel of the river until 1728 when it was replaced by the wider and deeper Smith's Leam, named after Humphrey Smith, a conservator of the Bedford Level. Morton's Leam is still where it was; but the original meandering, shifting channel below Peterborough, which the leam itself replaced, has disappeared.

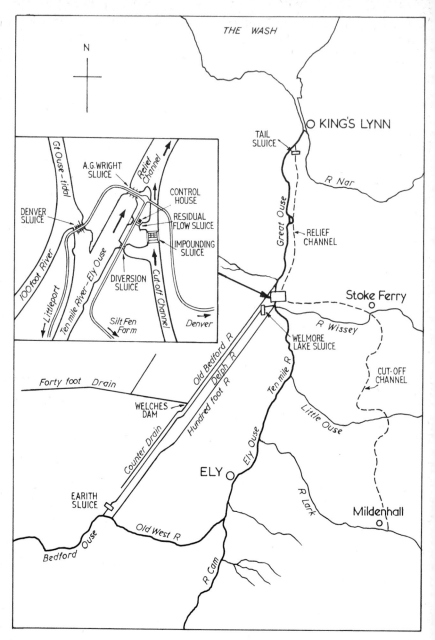

The Fenland River System

One of Cornelius Vermuyden's undertakings in his draining of the Fens was an improvement to Morton's Leam. Vermuyden was employed by the Earl of Bedford and his fellow 'adventurers' between 1630 and 1655 and engineered the cutting of a number of straight channels or drains. A look at the map shows how much he altered the landscape. His methods did not meet with everyone's approval; many other engineers believed that the answer lay in improving the capacity of the existing rivers rather than by creating new ones. But Vermuyden's work could not be undone. In after years the pattern he established could only be amended, added to, or improved upon where it fell short. The recent construction of the Cut-Off Channel around the eastern side of the Fens is the latest addition to the pattern; this takes off excess water from the upper reaches of the Ouse tributaries and also forms part of the inter-river transfer of water to Essex. When the Washlands between Vermuyden's two longest cuts, the Old and New Bedford rivers, are flooded, as they often are in the winter months, you can get some idea of what the Fenland would have looked like in the pre-drainage era.

The surplus water in the Fens was led off through interlocking systems of drains into straightened river channels leading to tidal outfalls. But this was not enough; often, to drain the land, the water had to be lifted from one level to another. At first this was done by a scoopwheel worked by man- or horse-power, until, during the sixteenth century, wind-operated waterpumps began to appear. These were adapted from corn-grinding windmills—sometimes they were called mills and sometimes engines. Of the several thousand that were built—there were over fifty in Whittlesea parish alone—there are only three survivors in East Anglia, at Wicken Fen in Cambridgeshire and at Horsey and Berney Arms in Norfolk. Windmills had two main disadvantages: they were unreliable, and farmers often had to stand by watching the waters covering their land while the mill stood idle, no wind blowing, and, as there was no controlling authority, anyone could set one up. As a result, one man's mill could destroy his neighbour's land; the records are full of cases where mill-owners were fined because their mills interfered with public drainage or damaged adjacent property.

Cheapness was the windmill's great advantage and it was this that seems to have delayed the introduction of steam engines. Newcomen engines were used to pump water out of mines in the early eighteenth century but many decades passed before serious thought was given to using steam power for land drainage. Then it was merely regarded as a supplement to wind power. Landowners had to realise that one large engine could do the work of several windmills, and the cost of fuel could

'Flood Protection, Navigation and Drainage': Langley Edwards's Report of 1771, one of several similar reports of the eighteenth and nineteenth centuries

be balanced by the saving of manpower, before the new method became acceptable. John Smeaton foresaw the time when the Fens would be drained by steam, but the first engineer to make really thorough and detailed recommendations was John Rennie. Between 1800 and 1820 he wrote about twenty reports on drainage and improvements in the Fens; few of his proposals were completed during his lifetime but many were put into effect after his death. Following 1817, about one engine a year was installed in the Fens—forty-one engines in thirty-five years.

Only two of the early steam engines that drained the Fens have been preserved. One is not far from Pode Hole, near Pinchbeck, north east of Spalding, where the Blue Gowt Drain meets Vernatt's Drain at a common outfall into the Welland. It worked from 1833 until 1952 and was the last steam engine to operate in the Fenland. The other, and larger, one is Stretham Old Engine, which raised water from the Waterbeach Level into the Old West River (part of the Great Ouse) from 1831 until 1925. From time to time it continued to work for a further sixteen years. Now it is in the care of the Stretham Engine Trust and can be inspected readily. You can still find some of the nineteenth-century engine houses, either derelict or with their pumps replaced by diesel or electrically driven machinery, but most of the smaller units have been replaced by fewer but more powerful engines housed in their own buildings.

Other areas reclaimed and drained include the Somerset marshes, on which work was being done in the tenth century. Glastonbury Abbey in particular undertook large-scale drainage operations and quadrupled the value of its Somerset estates by confining the rivers and digging ditches and drains—rhines is the local word—to take the water into them. In Sussex the dukes of Norfolk, throughout several centuries, have looked after the drainage in the valley of the Arun, their responsibilities, like those of other large landowners faced with similar problems, ending only with the creation of the Catchment Boards in 1930. Until recently drainage in this valley was virtually automatic, flap-valves in sluices being forced open when the water reached a certain level. Now small pumping stations have been built to provide more effective control. But no individual, institution, board or authority has made a greater alteration to the landscape or riverscape than did Vermuyden; stand between the bridges crossing the Old and New Bedford rivers and you will see his memorial.

One other function of the working river needs a mention. For water not only carried away waste—it carried away sin. The Ceiriog, a tributary of the Dee, was one of the rivers in which adult Baptists used to be totally immersed. No more do the faithful meet at Pontfadog to witness, or endure, the ceremony, but they used to do so until about 1939. George Borrow met a man who had enjoyed the benefit of this custom. 'On my telling him that I too had been baptized, he asked me if I had been dipped; and on learning that I had not, but only been sprinkled, according to the practice of my church, he gave me to understand that my baptism was not worth three halfpence.' Certainly there is no more beautiful a river to wash away one's sins than the Ceiriog in Denbighshire.

3

TRADES, CRAFTS AND PEOPLE

The first recorded use of the word 'waterman', according to the Oxford English Dictionary, was in 1458, defined as 'one who works on a boat'. 'Boatman'—'one who manages a boat'—dates from 1513. In 1608, watermen, boatmen, shipwrights and ship carpenters are all recorded in parishes on the banks of the Severn. By this time the Thames was a busy highway, and there were about 40,000 people gaining their living from working on boats between Windsor and Gravesend in the mid-seventeenth century. There was the same sort of competition between the various classes of watermen as there was between the pirate and official buses in the 1920s. There were the licensed 'common barges' sailing each tide and with an authorised fare. Competing with them were the tilt-boats—the tilt was an awning for the protection of passengers—which charged higher fares and which did not have to wait until the boat was full before departing. The tilt-boats eventually won over so many passengers that the common barges withdrew, whereupon they themselves were challenged by the wherries, light-horsemen and tide-boats, with still higher fares and fewer passengers, operating more like taxi-cabs than water-buses. All the watermen, however, were united in opposing the common enemy, the hackney-coach, against which they petitioned Parliament time after time, first to ban them and later to limit their use. It was a losing battle; by the end of the century many watermen had left the river and some of those remaining often had no more than one or two passenger trips a week.

In the interests of safety, watermen had to serve apprenticeships and to be examined before being admitted to the Watermen's Company. Even so, accidents were frequent, one of the worst occurring in 1698 when fifty-three out of sixty passengers were drowned when the Long Ferry tilt-boat capsized. At another capsize, when five people were drowned, the watermen, 'ungallant fellows, allowed themselves to be

50

saved'. So many accidents happened at London Bridge that passengers often demanded to be put ashore at Old Swan Stairs and would walk to a wharf on the other side of the bridge before returning to the boat.

The Thames watermen were not a popular crowd. Wye Saltonstall, writing in 1631, described the waterman as an 'embleame of deceite, for he rowes one way and lookes another'. 'When he comes ashore he mutinies,' said another critic, 'and contrary to all other trades is most surly to gentlemen, when they tender payment.' In return, John Taylor, who often acted as spokesman for his fellow-watermen, protested that the 'roaring boys' often swore at the watermen and then cheated them out of their fares. They were ready prey for the press-gangs, whose incursions often forced them off the river into hiding. In 1700 the lightermen, whose numbers were increasing as the quantity of goods handled in the Port of London increased, were enabled to join the Watermen's Company, which might otherwise have shrunk nearly to vanishing point as, with the improvements to roads, passenger-carrying by river became less and less important.

Elsewhere than in and around London the watermen, or bargemen as they were more commonly known, were not organised into a company and not subject to the same sort of regulations. What evidence there is shows that they were not a particularly popular body of men, although it is true that most of the complaints against them come from those who, for whatever reason, opposed river navigation itself. They had plenty of enemies, including millowners and riparian landowners; moreover, they also had to manage their 'halers'—those who towed the boats when they were unable to sail—who were likely to be casual labourers employed in this arduous and not especially rewarding task. On the Severn each vessel would usually have a crew of three or four, and there would be six or eight men hauling upstream. 'A degrading and unseemly' occupation was how Richard Reynolds, the ironmaster, described it. John Fletcher, vicar of Madeley for a time and a sympathiser with Methodism, asked how the bow-haulers differed from horses. 'Not in an erect posture of the body, for in the intenseness of the toil, they bend forward, their head is foremost, and their hand upon the ground. If there is any difference it consists in this: horses are indulged with a collar to save their breasts; and these; as if theirs were not worth saving draw without one; the beasts tug in patient silence and mutual harmony; but the men with loud contention and horrible imprecations.' Bow-hauling continued until the Severn towpaths were constructed, there still being a few at work in the mid-nineteenth century. A similar situation applied on the middle and upper reaches of

Bow-haulers at Isleworth in the mid-eighteenth century. The building facing downstream to the left of the church is the London Apprentice. The haulers, each attached to the rope by a leather strap, are reaching the end of their stint. They will return to Putney or Barnes by the next convenient vessel and another squad will take over, towing from the Middlesex bank. The engraving is from *The Modern Universal British Traveller*

the Thames, where the 'West Country' barges, as they were known, some of which approached 200 tons' burden, needed large gangs to haul them. When the Thames towpaths were made, it took about twelve horses to tow the larger West Country barges. There is evidence that men bow-hauled on the Lee, the Derbyshire Derwent, the Exe and the Bristol Avon; indeed, it is likely that they were used on almost all navigable rivers. Horses were much cheaper but needed established towing paths with gates or low stiles that could be easily negotiated. Constable's 'Leaping Horse' is leaping one of these barriers alongside the Suffolk Stour; this animal had an advantage over canal horses which could not be used in the Fens or East Anglia because they had not been trained to leap. On some waterways, notably the Broads, where there were no hauling paths, boats were poled or 'quanted' when they were unable to sail, but this method was not suitable for larger vessels, or for barges or lighters working in gangs. And evidence of another variety of motive power comes from an engraving published in 1792, where five animals—two horses and three oxen—are towing a boat along Cliveden Reach on the Thames. An engraving of the 1760s, from *England Display'd*, shows the superiority of the new canal navigation; two horses with ears pricked are trotting along towing two keels over the Barton aqueduct, while on the River Irwell beneath, two men on the bank, with the aid of a rope, are manoeuvring a much meaner-looking keel (under sail but apparently unmanned) under the centre arch of a quite absurd bridge.

Horses were used for towing on the Fen rivers earlier than on most—if not all—others. The horses were generally led by boys, whose lives were not always easy. They might have to lead their horses along submerged towpaths, or, if a staunch leaked, they might have to take a tarpaulin into the water to cover the hole. But the lives of the boatmen and haulers are poorly documented and the information that does turn up is usually only incidental.

Jackfield in the Severn Gorge was full of families who earned their living from the river and it seems to have been a fairly rowdy place; a commonplace book kept by a barge-owning family from 1828 to 1836 records several incidents of violence, slander and theft. But it is dangerous to generalise and it is not proven that bargemen and their fellow river-workers were any more prone to violence and dishonesty than other groups of workers. 'Although in their cups bargemen are sometimes quarrelsome,' said Henry Taunt, 'ordinarily they are quite as goodnatured & obliging as the majority of the working classes.'

The censuses in the reign of Victoria show the numbers of those

Canal and River contrast: view of part of the Duke of Bridgewater's Navigation across the Irwell

employed in inland navigation averaging about 30,000, while those employed in the railway service increased from 2,000 in 1841 to 186,900 in 1891. It is not possible to differentiate between workers on rivers and workers on canals; indeed, a great many men worked on both. 'Pride of the Thames', the frontispiece to H. R. Robertson's *Life on the Upper Thames*, published 1875, shows 'the fair steerer' of a canal boat, the title of the picture being also the name of the boat. Stourport on the Severn was an important meeting-place for river and canal traffic, with locks for barges and for narrow boats and four basins above the river.

There are two trades connected especially with the sailing barges of the Thames and Medway. On these tidal rivers barges frequently came to rest on the ground, and some wharfingers used to make barge beds on which a hull could sink to rest as the tide ebbed. These beds were edged with timber—perhaps old mainmasts—and had to be kept in good order or the wharfinger would be liable for damage. So luters were employed, men who waded into the water and smoothed the mud in the barge beds so that the hulls would lie easy.

The other specialist was the huffler, who came on board to help work barges up the Medway or Darent. He might act as a river pilot for a skipper who was new to the particular river. But his main job was to help lower and raise the mast for the barge to pass under the bridges. He would stand on the huff—the overhanging section of the bow of a swim-headed river barge—and at the critical moment would ease away the stayfall so that the mast with spars and canvas would be lowered onto the hatches and the bridge would be shot. When the mast was raised again, the huffler would get back into his rowing boat and return to land, his fee—five shillings (25p) for the two bridges at Rochester—in his pocket. Many skippers sailed their barges single-handed, with the help only of a huffler for the occasional bridge.

Obviously, the major riverside trade was boat-building and, until recently, boats were built in yards alongside the river on which they were going to be used. By the Trent the main boat-building centres were Newark and Nottingham; about one-third of the Trent barges came from these yards between the mid-eighteenth and mid-nineteenth centuries. The Barnsdall family ran five yards in Nottingham, Newark and Loughborough on the Soar. In this period only two boats are recorded as having been built for carriage of passengers on the Trent. There were boatyards at seven places at least on the Yorkshire Ouse, including York. On the Great Ouse, boats were built at St Ives, Ely and King's Lynn, on the Little Ouse at Thetford, on the Cam at Cambridge, and lighters were built at Burwell at the head of the Lode. On the Severn, trows were built at Tewkesbury and at other places on the lower river including Newnham and Chepstow on the Wye; smaller craft were built at yards in the Severn Gorge. Sailing flats were built at Winsford and Northwich on the Weaver, and keels at several yards in Yorkshire and Lincolnshire, at Beverley, New Holland, Thorne, Barton-on-Humber and Stanley Ferry among other places.

On the middle and upper Thames there were many boatyards. The earlier commercial barges were cumbersome, straight-sided, punt-ended craft with a short mast that could be lowered to pass under bridges. They could take a small square sail, similar in shape to a keel's. With the opening of the Thames & Severn Canal, Samuel Bird established a boatyard at The Bourne, near Brimscombe. In 1790 he produced his first barge, influenced by the hull shape of the Severn trow, with the sides more rounded, a definite bow and stern (with the earlier barges it is difficult sometimes to tell from illustrations which way they were going) and decking at each end. Yards at Abingdon, Pangbourne and Reading followed his example, and soon this type of vessel was common on the river.

Most of the riverside boatyards were small concerns, building only one boat at a time. Such were most of the yards in Norfolk and Suffolk,

W. REDKNAP, Queen's Waterman, by Appointment.

MEAKES & REDKNAP,
ENGINEERS,
STEAM LAUNCH AND BOAT BUILDERS,
BRIDGE WORKS AND VICTORIA BOAT HOUSES
(ABOVE BRIDGE),
GREAT MARLOW.

STEAM LAUNCHES (ALL SIZES), HOUSE BOATS, ROWING BOATS, PUNTS, CANOES, ETC., OF EVERY DESCRIPTION, **LET ON HIRE BY THE HOUR, DAY, WEEK, MONTH, OR SEASON.**

Gentlemen's Boats attended to, Housed, Repaired, and Varnished.

DRESSING ROOMS, LAVATORIES, AND EVERY CONVENIENCE FOR LADIES AND GENTLEMEN BOATING.

Steam Launches taken out of the water on Improved Slip-ways, for Repairs, or Housed for the Winter.

Repairs, Alterations, and Additions of all kinds undertaken; also Painting and Varnishing.

STEAM-LAUNCH REQUISITES KEPT.

The British Pure Ice Company's Ice can always be had at the Boat Houses, in small or large quantities, at Reasonable Prices.

Pending the completion of our Works and Boat Houses we have taken the River Frontage of the "Anglers" Hotel, where Boats of all kinds will be taken in and Let throughout the season.

The great advantage of both our Boat House and "Anglers" Hotel Frontages is, they are on the private side of the river, so that our patrons will be saved the annoyance of the public towing-path.

P.S.—A Boat always in readiness to fetch Ladies and Gentlemen across from the Towing-path opposite our Boat Houses.

Telegrams:—MEAKES REDKNAP, MARLOW.

Advertisement from Taunt's Map of the Thames

56

Boat-building at Carrow, on the Yare, 1834

where wherries and smaller craft were built, often of locally grown timber. There were several yards in Norwich, one of them William Petch's in Barrack Street, with others in the King Street vicinity. James Stark drew a wherry being built at Carrow in the 1830s, four men being involved in the construction. There were yards at Bungay and Beccles, Barton Staithe, Thorpe and Oulton Broad, as well as at the ports of Yarmouth and Lowestoft. One of the last of the traditional yards to survive was Allen's on the Bure at Coltishall, run by the family from 1864 until 1974. The last wherry from here was launched in 1912. Like most other yards, Allen's employed only about half a dozen men, and much of their time was spent in maintaining and repairing.

The most local of boat-builders are probably the coracle-makers of the Severn, Teify, Tavy and Taff. These little portable craft, 5-6ft long, were usually made for an individual owner—almost tailor-made, one might say. The Severn coracle was shaped like a bowl, with a paddle similar to a canoe paddle, usually made of ash. They were popular in the Gorge as they enabled local inhabitants to cross the river without having to pay the penny toll for using the Iron Bridge. In flood-time they were used for catching rabbits. William Gilpin found coracles in use on the Wye in 1770, and reported on one famous voyage as follows:

An adventurous fellow, for a wager, once navigated a coricle as far as the isle of Lundy, at the mouth of the Bristol channel. A full fortnight or more he spent in this dangerous voyage; and it was happy for him that it was a fortnight of serene weather . . . Sometimes his little bark was carried far to windward, and sometimes as far to leeward; but still he recovered his course; persevered in his undertaking; and at length happily achieved it. When he returned to New-Weir, report says, the account of his expedition was received like a voyage round the world.

Gilpin describes the coracle as constructed 'of waxed canvas stretched over a few slight ribs'. They were built rather like a basket, of willow laths with, in earlier years, hide, and later calico, nailed over them.

In southern England, there were boatyards at Pallingham on the Arun and at Arundel. On the various isolated river navigations, barges were built locally to suit the dimensions of the local navigation. Near Flatford Mill on the Stour, Golding Constable owned a convenient dry dock for barges' which he inherited with other property in 1764. Here he built the barges which carried flour from his mill down the river to Mistley and brought back coal and other goods. This is the boatyard painted by his son John in 1814, a picture exhibited in the Royal

Coracle fisherman with his craft, on the Teify near Cenarth

Academy the following year. Many of the barges in Constable's paintings must have been built here. Constable is said to have painted this particular picture entirely in the open air. It is a worthy monument to all those builders of wooden riverboats who worked without drawings or plans, relying on the judgement of the eye and the skill of the hand.

Few boats are built of wood in the present day and there are few survivors from times past. One wooden fen lighter and one wooden Stour barge have recently been salvaged and restored, and it is hoped that the Chepstow-built trow *Spry* can be rescued. There are a few wooden-hulled Thames and Medway sailing barges, some of which can be seen at Maldon and Pin Mill on the Orwell. And there are still plenty of wooden punts, especially at Oxford and Cambridge. Are any of them survivors from the late nineteenth century when Harry Tagg, among many others, was building mahogany punts 'of 26 feet length, inclusive of two poles, rep lounge cushion, and burdens throughout' from 20 guineas each? The hulls of today's river craft are made of steel or glass reinforced fibre; they are the work of the technician rather than the craftsman.

Boat-building is not the only riverside craft that has declined. One of the oldest crafts is basket-making, still given its chapter in books devoted to rural crafts, although it lacks the popular appeal of country pottery or wood-turning, or the nostalgic fascination of thatching. Osiers—the willow, usually *Salix viminalis* used in basket-work—used to be common in Somerset, Essex, the north, where the osier-beds were known as garths, and in the Midlands where they were called holts or hams. It was an important local industry alongside the Kennet in Berkshire, on the upper Thames, the Trent and by some Scottish rivers. H. R. Robertson quotes an 'animated description' of osier-cutting on the Trent:

> The osier-cutters were up with the lark; and while the morning dew hung like pearls on the graceful willows, did they march with hooks in their hands; and taking stock by stock, and row by row, level all their new-budding and leafy honours with the ground; and laying bare many a half-finished bird's-nest, which was before shrouded by its tall tuft of nodding osiers. What a gap have they already made, through ground so thickly planted, that, an hour before, the eye could not penetrate many feet from the footpath! And those tall osiers, many of them from ten to twelve, and even fifteen feet high, are but the growth of a single year. Twelve months ago, and those stocks or stems, standing but a foot high, were as round and naked as those which were this morning cut; and yet many of them have borne scores of osiers, not a few of which measure the full length we

have stated. Osier-cutting is the hardest work—stooping from morning until night, and bending down the tall-headed willows with one hand, whilst the other wields the ponderous and sharp-edged hook, a cut from which will never be forgotten, should it glance from the stock and alight upon either leg or arm.

On both Trent and Thames the osiers after cutting were sorted into four groups according to size, the names for the different-sized rods, in ascending order, being Luke, Threepenny, Middleborough and Great. By 1875 a bolt (or bundle) of Threepenny was worth about one shilling and threepence (6p). Men did the cutting, but the stripping or peeling was usually undertaken by women or girls. Robertson mentions an American invention 'worked by horse or steam power' which was rumoured to be able to strip a ton of rods a day. Stripping machines were introduced in later years, and rods were sent to factories to be stripped instead of worked at home, by hand or through springs made from steel rods.

You can see the remains of osier-beds by many rivers and streams; low stumps growing in wet ground, with branches of willow springing from them. Untended, they now provide useful cover for wild birds. By the late 1960s nearly all England's commercial willow-growing was concentrated in Somerset near the River Parrett, where in 1969 there were about 850 acres of willows. In a single acre there might be 17,000 plants. Wicker furniture and baskets are among the more usual end-products; the thickest osier could form the leg of a wicker chair or small table. Most of the sticks were sent to be made up elsewhere, but here and there basket-making still survives as an unmechanised cottage industry, with the old tools used in the old ways.

Eel-traps made of osiers were used on both the Thames and the Severn. On the Thames they were called grig-weels (a small eel on the Thames was known as a grig) or eel-bucks, similar in construction but the bucks being larger. Sometimes gudgeon were used as bait. On the Severn the basketwork traps were called putcheons or weels, the latter being the larger. As bait, a piece of rabbit or lamprey might be used. In recent decades, galvanised iron and wire netting have replaced basketwork in eel-traps. Lampreys and lamperns, which in the Middle Ages were delicacies particularly favoured by royalty (Henry I is said to have died from a surfeit of them and both John and Henry III are known to have enjoyed them), used to be caught in traps similar to those used for eels; they were stored and transported in baskets submerged in water.

Basketwork is also used in trapping salmon. Stakes were placed across

(*above*) Osier cutting on the Upper Thames, 1875;
(*below*) lowering eel-bucks, described as 'rough filters, which permit
the water to run through but retain the fish'. They were mounted on a
'stage', usually placed where the current was strong between an island
and the river bank

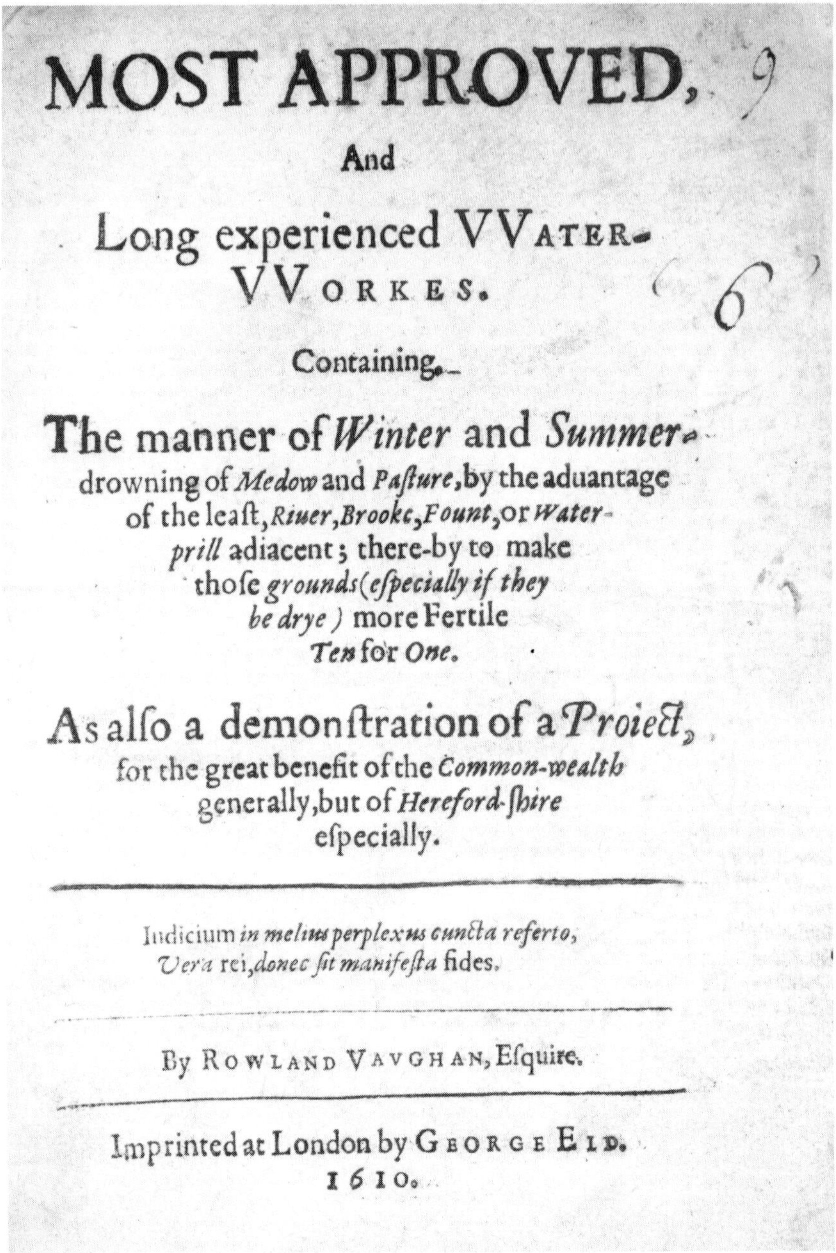

MOST APPROVED, *9*

And

Long experienced VVater-VVorkes. *6*

Containing.

The manner of *Winter* and *Summer*-
drowning of *Medow* and *Pasture*, by the aduantage
of the least, *Riuer*, *Brooke*, *Fount*, or *Water-*
prill adiacent; there-by to make
those *grounds* (*especially if they*
be drye) more Fertile
Ten for One.

As also a demonstration of a *Proiect*,
for the great benefit of the *Common-wealth*
generally, but of *Hereford-shire*
especially.

Iudicium in melius perplexus cuncta referto,
Vera rei, donec sit manifesta fides.

By ROWLAND VAVGHAN, Esquire.

Imprinted at London by GEORGE ELD.
1610.

Title-page of Rowland Vaughan's *Water-Workes*

channels of the tidal Severn and putchers or putts arranged between them. Putchers are cones of loose basketwork up to 6ft long; a putcher weir might consist of three rows extending a considerable distance into the river, say 50yd long and 10ft high. The putt is much larger than the putcher; they would be laid in single rows and facing upstream. At the thin end, the basketwork is closely woven so that the smallest fish could be retained. Being too cumbersome to be removed from the river in the close season, the putts could be sealed off against salmon by two rods being driven into them halfway along. Putts have a long history, but putchers seem to date from the nineteenth century. Since 1865 the numbers of fishing weirs used have been subject to regulation.

Many crafts and trades grew up along riversides because of the availability of transport rather than for any other reason. With the decline of commercial carrying these trades declined also, or moved elsewhere. For a time the Wye was famous, not only for its dramatic scenery and Tintern Abbey, but for the foundries and wire works between Monmouth and Chepstow. In South Wales the valleys provided the sites for industry but the rivers themselves, although they could supply water for power, were impossible as navigations. For transport to the developing ports on the Bristol Channel, heavily locked canals were cut; the Swansea Canal in the Tawe valley, the Glamorganshire Canal alongside the Taff from Merthyr Tydfil to Cardiff, and the Brecon & Abergavenny and Monmouthshire canals, meeting end-on by Pontypool, running roughly parallel to the Usk and descending to the level of its estuary at Newport. On the estuaries of these and greater rivers the docks were extended, ship-building became a major occupation and heavy industries developed; above the tidal reaches the rivers had their own qualities of rural tranquillity.

In earlier years, commercial freshwater fisheries were of great importance to the national economy, not only in estuaries but in upper reaches as well. As well as the construction of fish weirs the making of nets and implements such as eel-spears were riverside activities. Net-making is one of the oldest of crafts, but today it is associated with fishing ports rather than riversides, although eel-nets were certainly being knitted by the Severn in the 1950s.

A craft which has been recently revived is the management of water meadows, which introduces us to the skills of the 'floater' or 'drowner'. This involves the controlled irrigation of grasslands, not simply by abstraction and sprinkling, but by the construction of sluices and cutting of trenches in appropriate patterns so that water may be let in and run off at the desired times. The method was in use on the English-

Rowland Vaughan's Project. A stream runs straight through the dining-room, turns the wheel of the mill and continues through the slaughter house. The square of buildings is composed of 'tenements for Artifycers'; above is the garden

Welsh border in the late sixteenth century, when one of its practitioners was Rowland Vaughan, of New Court near Peterchurch in Herefordshire, who described his undertakings in a book, *The Most Approved and Long Experienced Water-Workes*, published in 1610. Vaughan, born in 1559, went to live on his wife's estate in 'the Golden-Vale, the Lombardy of Herefordshire, the Garden of the Old Gallants and Paradice of the backside of the Principallitee', where he built a mill 'governed by a little Bastard-Brooke, fedde with eight living Springs . . . to grinde mine owne Corne', and where he claimed to have founded his own commonwealth, dependent on the use of water power for a variety of purposes.

Vaughan claimed to have got the idea of his waterworks from seeing a stream issuing from a molehill on the bank of a brook and noticing the improvement it made to the ground along its course. Presumably it was the Dore river—or a stream leading into it—that he used for irrigating his meadows and where he placed his 'commanding Weare or Scluce'. His works covered over 300 acres, including his main trench—or 'Trench-royall'—and his 'counter-trenches, depending-trenches, topping or braving-trenches, Winter and Summer-trench, double and treble-trenches, a traversing trench with a point, and an ever-lasting trench, with other troublesome trenches . . .'. The main trench was 3 miles long, 16ft broad and 8ft deep for the first half-mile and 10ft broad, 4ft deep for the remainder. On his trenches he floated two little boats for carrying earth, but he saw the potential passenger-carrying use of the system 'if any man be so phantasticall as to carry his wife levell by water to her Dairy'.

When the system was being constructed, Vaughan's carpenter put the main sluice across the river supported by about 1,000 stakes. Vaughan objected to this method, saying that the water would undermine the sill, but the carpenter 'grew teasty, hott and peremptory; and sayd it was not the Maister's manner to controule; but to examine; and that all his Water-workes were according to the Venetian foundation, built altogether upon Piles; but the Venetian-fashion forced mee to want water ten yeares space, which was out of my way two thousand pounds'. Nevertheless, Vaughan increased the value of his land from £40 to £300 a year. At the end of his book he must have realised that his descriptions of his waterworks may not have been made completely clear, as he invited his readers to meet him for an explanation in London, 'and for a Supper, at John Gents you shall have your Belly-full of Water-workes'.

The term 'water meadows' is usually applied to grassland adjacent to streams and rivers which is naturally flooded in winter. Vaughan's were

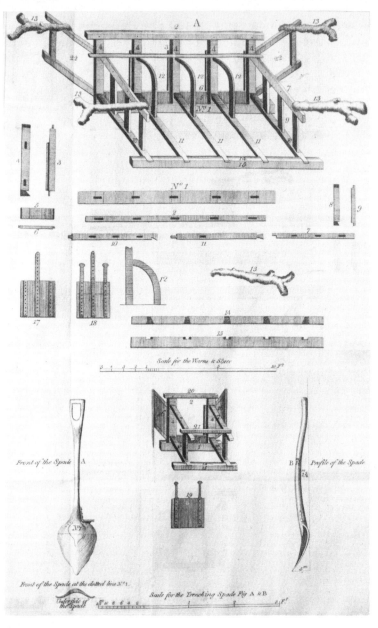

Illustration of the various components of a 'ware' (top) and sluice (bottom) from George Boswell's *Treatise on Watering Meadows*, 1792, 3rd edition

upland meadows, and he was applying art to what occurred by nature in the lower reaches. His example was followed by the earls of Pembroke on their chalklands on Salisbury Plain, and the floating of meadows spread through Wiltshire to Berkshire, Dorset, Hampshire, the Midlands and eastern England; among the rivers whose water was used were the Itchen, Hampshire Avon, Kennet, Frome and Exe. Water was let into the meadows in November, when the sluice was closed on the main stream and the water was diverted along a main trench and into subsidiary trenches which were lined with timber. It covered the meadows completely, fertilising them with chalk and other deposits and protecting the grass from frost. By the middle of March the grass was up to 6in tall; the water was drained off and, a few days later, sheep were let in to graze. Later the meadows could again be floated for a few days and then put up for hay or grazed by cattle. After this, the system was cleaned out for the winter floating.

In 1779 George Boswell, who farmed in Piddletown, Dorset, published his *Treatise on Watering Meadows*, which ran into three editions and gives a clear and well illustrated account of the practice. His terminology is less poetic than Rowland Vaughan's but his instructions are much more specific. Some idea of the extent of the system in Dorset is gained from his mention that there were at least 500 weirs or sluices within 7 miles of Dorchester. Arthur Young, in his *General View of the Agriculture of Norfolk*, was disappointed to find how few farmers were irrigating their meadows in this way. But some farmers were beginning to show interest, and Mr Brooks, from Gloucestershire, presumably a 'floater' or 'drowner', was called in to advise some of them. On one particular farm Brooks discovered the foundations of an old sluice and the carriers and drains which had been 'utterly neglected for at least 80 years. . . . It is extremely curious', commented Young, 'thus to trace former exertions in so excellent a husbandry, followed by so long a period of darkness and ignorance, as to suffer such immense advantages to sink into a state of neglect and ruin.' Young, as Vaughan before him, saw the millers as opponents of floating meadows, and he criticised proprietors for muddling themselves in the low flat lands when they should be 'Running levels as high as possible for floating the dry arable', and making pounds instead of shillings. Should any 'lousy miller . . . yelp at the undertaking' the proprietors 'should unite and buy, or burn, the mills, before they think of beginning'.

While it was generally considered that the floating of meadows more than doubled their value, this system of irrigation, although it endured into the twentieth century, has almost disappeared. It needed the skill of the floater or drowner, and this breed of craftsman—we can imagine him with his line and reel and his 'stout large Water-Boots . . . large enough to admit a quantity of hay to be stuffed down all round the legs, and be kept well tallowed, to resist the running water for eight, nine and ten hours together'—has died out. Moreover, floating of meadows often needed the co-operation of the neighbouring farmer; it also affected fishing, and as fishing rights rose in value the interest of the sport sometimes became predominant. The importing of cheap animal food diminished the demand for high quality grazing, and the increasing use of artificial fertilisers made the system unnecessary or impractical. Here and there, however, farms can still be found where water meadows are used in the traditional way; one example is on George Boswell's home ground in Dorset, watered by the Devil's Brook on the system laid out about two centuries ago.

Returning to the rivers themselves, we can look at some of the people

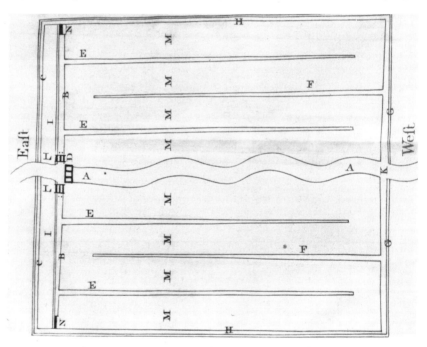

Plan of a meadow watered on each side of a stream, from Boswell's *Treatise*. LL are the weirs admitting water into the mains (BB) and thence into the trenches (EE). M indicates the grass-bearing meadow-land

who have devoted their lives and derived their livelihoods directly from their service. George and John Siddons, father and son, may stand as examples of the old school of river surveyors and engineers. For eighty years they worked for the commissioners of the River Nene, a body with a chronic shortage of funds responsible for a heavily locked river subject to frequent floods. A few years after his appointment as surveyor, George was asked to agree to a reduction in his salary to £100 a year, which he accepted. As some compensation he was granted the management of the tolls on the river for an extra £40 a year. The commissioners owned a dredger which they let out for hire when they might have been using it on their own river. George struggled on, doing his best to maintain the river with a small staff, defending them against attacks from the millers—Mr Jelly's employees at Yarwell Mill were particularly obstreperous—and doing his best to keep the locks and staunches in working order while trying to ensure that the few traders using the navigation duly paid their tolls. Then the dredger sunk off the Suffolk coast, on its way to Maldon; the Peterborough toll-collector decamped, having embezzled £4 11s 8d (£4.59); George was asked to find appropriate employment for R. Stephens, a regular workman for the commissioners but now 'aged and infirm' at 10s (50p) a week; twenty-nine Thrapston householders complained about the state of the river, and the Ecclesiastical Commissioners were reluctant to repair their waste gates at Alwalton; the commissioners decided they could no longer afford to supply their workmen with ale except in cases of emergency and then only by the written order of Mr Siddons. So it went on; Mr Cornwell's horse was drowned, his appeal for a replacement was rejected and he was ordered to remove his sunken lighter near Barnwell Mill; obstructions in the river below Peterborough, outside Siddons's area, contributed to flooding and added to the problems. In 1880 George asked the commissioners if his son John could be associated with him in his duties. They agreed, appointing him acting deputy surveyor—as long as he did not ask to be paid. Father and son accepted, and for nine years John worked without pay until his father died in 1889 and John succeeded him.

John struggled on, as his father had done before him, careful and conscientious. Commercial traffic was falling off and John suggested reducing the tolls to retain some of the trade. But coal to Billing went by rail; the through timber-carrying came to an end, the Elton gravel pits closed, and W. Cornwell's gang of lighters, loaded with slag, were carried away in floods and ended up in a meadow. Pleasure boats were coming onto the Nene but were causing more problems as they damaged the locks through being carelessly handled. Nevertheless, in 1893, John could report several improvements; gates had been made to replace horse leaps; horse bridges built over tributaries, and bricks were imported from Staffordshire for lock repairs. In the next year there were sixty pleasure boats on hire at Northampton, and the boaters had obtained keys to the padlocks on the slackers so that they were using the river without payment. Siddons brought in a permit system to control pleasure traffic, which seemed to work. In 1897, when 'a new foreman was needed at Wellingborough, he commented on the changing attitudes of river workmen; there was difficulty in finding a working foreman of the old type, 'as those who can write and figure seem to have an increasing objection to the heavy and dirty work that falls to the leading man on any work such as those carried out by the commissioners'. Nevertheless, when Henry de Salis inspected the river in the same year he found the locks and waterway generally 'in a very fair state of repair'.

As well as looking after the long and tortuous river, John Siddons was a member of the Oundle UDC and the Oundle Rowing Club. He cared for the interests of his subordinates, often intervening with the commissioners on their behalf. He was concerned about the boatmen who drank throughout Saturdays, began their journeys on Sundays when there was no toll-collector on duty and tended to fall in the river, some of them being drowned.

The year 1914 was a very bad year for the Nene, with shortage of water and very little flow in the summer months. There is a note of despair in John's comment in his report: 'The Mill owners complain of the Boatmen and the Bargemen complain of the Millers—both want compensation and it has been the most trying quarter I have known.' His problems were accentuated by difficulties with a married couple, Mr and Mrs Tooley, who were fined for leaving a lighter all night in Houghton locks and then for breaking padlocks on the lock gates. John's workmen complained to him of the foul language used by the Tooleys every time they passed them. 'It was bad in years gone by,' they said, 'but it has been almost unbearable since they were fined.' The Tooleys then refused to lock up the padlocks after use; troubles with them are recorded for another six years.

Shortage of labour during the war caused John yet more problems. In 1917 he reported that it had not been possible to cut the weeds for three years and that it took four hours to haul a boat loaded with clay a distance of just over a mile. In 1920 it took a week for a small motor boat to cover the 65 miles between Peterborough and Northampton, with Siddons's men having to help drag the boat overland several times.

John completed fifty years' service on the Nene in 1926. He thanked the commissioners for their kindness and consideration. 'I have thoroughly enjoyed my work,' he wrote. 'My one regret is to see the condition of the River deteriorating through lack of sufficient funds.' But the really troubled times were nearly over. The Land Drainage Act of 1930 brought river Catchment Boards into being and opened various ways of raising money for river improvements. George Dallas was appointed chairman of the Nene Board and Harold Clark its engineer. Large-scale works began, including dredging, widening and the rebuilding of the locks, 'magnificent . . . solid-looking things in Haunchwood brick and concrete', as well as the replacement of the staunches by pound locks. John Siddons was present at a luncheon during an inspection day of the river in 1936. 'In the whole country,' said George Dallas, 'there is not a single solitary person who knows more about the work and troubles and problems of the River Nene than Mr Siddons.' In his reply, John spoke with some emotion: 'I am sure you will not judge me too harshly when you see the state of the river and the locks and some of the works, seeing that the amount allotted to me for the 65½ miles between Peterborough Bridge and Northampton was the munificent sum of £1,300 a year, to carry out all the repairs, so that my task has not been a very enviable one. . . . Although there has been no record of wonderful works carried out,' he continued, 'I think there is no record of my having neglected my duty . . . I believe your oldest foreman has worked for me ever since he was a boy, as also did his father and grandfather, so we have had some very happy relations both with the men and with the Commissioners.' He ended his speech with just a touch of bitterness. 'I regret I had not the happy wand to get money from the Government as you have done. They offered me the magnificent sum of £500 after the war to add to the £1,300!'

River service often inspired a devotion that was handed down through generations, whether the actual occupation was maintenance and engineering, lock-keeping, boat-building or working boats themselves. On the Thames the families of Phelps and Turk are examples; on the Cam there were the Dants and on the Ely Ouse the Appleyards. East Anglia in particular seems to have a special breed of inland watermen, although in their lifetimes the present heads of the families have seen the decline and disappearance of the trading by which they used to live. Not so long ago, Ely was the centre of a flourishing waterborne trade, many of the lighters in which the goods were carried being built by the Appleyards. As trade fell away, the boatyard was taken over by Harry

Lincoln, who had himself worked boats since the age of fourteen. Ted Appleyard became skipper of the little oil tanker *Shellfen*, which supplied fuel to many of the pumping stations in the Middle Level. So bad were conditions in Well Creek one Christmas that Ted had to get out of *Shellfen* and try to push her through the mud. The boatyard turned to the production of pleasure cruisers but eventually succumbed to rising prices and VAT and went into liquidation.

The Fen watermen certainly worked extremely hard. The Doubledays of Outwell are an example. Lou Doubleday's grandfather was a lighterman and captain of a steam tug; Lou himself has worked all his life to keep boats moving on the Fens, knowing the Wash and the rivers intimately and helping with enthusiasm to encourage and assist pleasure boaters when the day of the lighters ended. The Jacksons of Stanground and March are another well known family. Vic worked lighters from Stanground, and Archie and another brother from March; their father was a barge-owner and lighterman. By the time he was twenty-eight, Vic owned twenty barges and a steam tug. He traded on the Nene, the Middle Level Navigations, the Great Ouse and its tributaries and on the Cambridgeshire lodes; as a lad, he took the last pair of barges through the Wisbech Canal before it was abandoned. When delivering fertiliser to farms along the waterways, Vic did not stop his gang; he would jump off with the sacks on his shoulders, dump them and jump back on further along the train for more if necessary. Vic had little patience with authority; he demolished fences that obstructed his horses on the halingways, winning a court case that was brought against him as a consequence, and once, exasperated when his lighters were delayed overlong at March through shortage of water, he got on his bicycle at night and, in a furious temper, cycled up the halingways as far as he could, drawing every sluice he came to, so that by morning there was enough water to float his gang off. There was also enough water to cover several hundred acres where it wasn't wanted!

When the trading diminished, Vic started boat-building and making conversions from wooden lifeboats; he also went into road-haulage. His yard still flourishes, near the yard of the Lees, also famous lightermen in their time.

The last few decades have seen great changes in the work done on and by the rivers and in the types of people that earn their living thereby. Phelps's yard still makes wooden boats at Putney, but more and more boatyards have gone over to GRP or steel hulls and mass production means fewer and larger units, sometimes situated surprisingly far from water. There are no lightermen in the Fens and few enough on the tidal

Thames, as containerisation takes over. Mostly those who navigate the non-tidal reaches of rivers do so for pleasure and not for profit, and the same can be said for those who fish in them, except where prize money is at stake. It is still possible to find an old lock-keeper 'with a tale to tell' but it becomes more difficult yearly. There are a few osier-cutters, and you may even find a floater or a drowner—but not many. There are engineers and scientists, however, naturalists and conservationists, and any number of environmentalists. And if you are lucky you may even find a Regional Water Authority Recreational Officer! That should be glory enough for anyone.

4

RIVERS AS HIGHWAYS

'River navigation', wrote Professor T. S. Willan, 'is as old as civilization itself.' We know that in Britain the Romans used certain rivers for navigation, including the Trent and the Yorkshire Ouse. But there seems no way of telling which of our rivers was the first to be navigated, although in medieval times the Severn, Thames, Great Ouse, Trent, Humber, Yorkshire Ouse and several other connecting Yorkshire rivers were all regularly navigable for much of their length. And among other rivers used as trading routes by the early seventeenth century were the lower reaches of the Dee, Parrett, Bristol Avon, Exe, Warwickshire Avon, Kentish Stour, Medway, Wey, Lee, Yare, Cam, Little Ouse, Nene and Tyne. As John Taylor wrote to the burgesses of Salisbury in 1623, 'in the whole dominion of England, there is not one Towne or City which hath a Navigable River at it, that is poore, nor scarce any that are rich, which want a River with the Benefit of Boats. . . .' Taylor could have quoted many other examples, including York to the north, Worcester and Gloucester to the west and Cambridge to the east. Near Cambridge, Stourbridge, one of the great fairs of the Middle Ages, received much of its supplies by water, as did Reach, site of another major fair, at the end of Reach Lode, a tributary of the Cam. Most of the other large fairs were held at places where there was easy access from navigable rivers: among them London, Bristol, Exeter, Chester, St Ives on the Great Ouse, Boston and Edinburgh.

Before the development of canals and the improvement in roads—both occurring in the second half of the eighteenth century—rivers were very important in the economy of the country. Coastal vessels brought goods to ports situated on estuaries, where they were transhipped and carried inland by smaller vessels—keels on the Humber, trows on the Severn, barges on the Thames, or lighters in the Fenland. The rivers were common highways, but the condition of the navigation was the

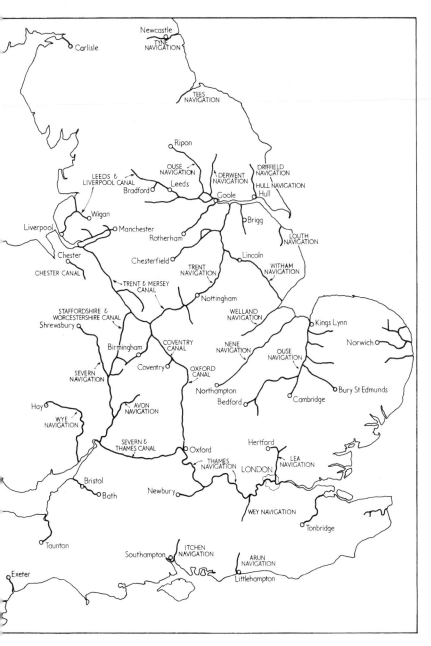

Map of the Waterway System, 1789

75

responsibility of nobody. The various commissions of sewers were concerned only with the drainage of a particular area; millowners were interested only in the supply of water to their mills, and sometimes in the netting or trapping of fish. Weirs, dams and nets obstructed the navigation and appeal against them, to be effective, had to be made to the king. From the time of Edward the Confessor onward there are frequent references to nuisances caused by obstructions to navigation. In the reign of Edward III two Acts were passed concerning obstructions and the setting up or enlarging of weirs, which recalled provisions in Magna Carta for the removal of weirs on all rivers, the Thames and Medway being specifically referred to. It was not that weirs in themselves were necessarily always detrimental to navigation; indeed, they were often positively helpful by building up a level of water which enabled boats to pass over shallows. Rather was the objection to the attitude of the millowners in operating the weirs for their own benefit and refusing speedy passage to boats or charging excessive tolls. It is interesting to see how some of the earlier Acts refer to the antiquity of navigation; an Act of Henry VII declares that the Severn had been used by merchants and others since 'time out of mind', and a much later Act passed in 1750 says that the Thames from London to Burcot and from Oxford to beyond Lechlade had been navigable 'from time immemorial'. The early navigability of three other rivers—the Great Ouse, the Witham and the Kentish Stour—is evidenced by the use made of them by the Danes as routes to Ely, Lincoln and Canterbury which they burnt. They penetrated the Ouse as far inland as Willington, 5 miles east of Bedford, where they built a harbour, probably a few years after they had sailed up the Lee to Hertford in 894.

The Lee indeed was one of the first rivers to be dealt with by particular legislation. An Act for the Preservation of the River Lee was passed in 1425 and a further Act in the reign of Elizabeth I proposed to improve the navigation of the river by making an artificial cut on the north side of London. A strange feature in the history of river improvement, however, is the failure, for nearly two hundred years, to make much use of the pound lock, introduced into England by John Trew, engineer of the Exeter Ship Canal which was opened in 1566. The canal was constructed by the corporation to overcome the blocking of the river by the Courtenays, earls of Devon, who installed weirs, forcing boats to unload at Topsham where the Courtenays owned the quay and took tolls. Trew built his canal on the east side of the river; it was originally 1 ¾ miles long (since extended to 5 miles) and only 16ft wide at the surface. Three locks were built, with guillotine-type gates; masts

Boats on the Thames in the time of Victoria

had to be lowered to pass under them. These locks were replaced by the double locks when the canal was improved in 1701. The use of pound locks was slow to develop, the Lee, Trent and Thames being among rivers where they sporadically appeared. Arnold Spencer's sluices on the upper Great Ouse, installed between 1618 and 1630, were probably pound locks.

Spencer's work on the Great Ouse was undertaken on the terms of letters patent granted to him by the Crown, under which he was allowed to make any rivers navigable during a period of eleven years. For this he was to pay the exchequer £5 a river, while in return he was to receive all the profits for eighty years. The Great Ouse was the only river he seems to have improved. Other rivers made navigable by letters patent included the Warwickshire Avon, the Soar, Tone and Lark, though not all the work was necessarily completed, nor did the rivers always remain navigable for very long. Until the Restoration few rivers were improved by Act of Parliament; following the measure for the Lee, there was only a handful of Acts passed until 1662. Then legislation began in earnest; by 1745, improvement Acts were passed for a total of forty-two rivers, including such apparently minor examples as the Dane, Eden, Idle, Itchen, Mole, Salwarpe and the Worcestershire Stour. To these we can add a number of rivers naturally navigable, of which the Severn is the best example; indeed, most of the earlier legislation regarding the Severn concerned the towing-path rather than the channel of the river itself.

Between 1660 and 1724 the total length of river navigation in England increased from 685 miles to 1,160 miles. By now pound locks were becoming more common; the Kennet, Stroudwater, Don and Colne were some of the rivers where they were constructed. In the next few years the Dee and the Mersey underwent major improvements. Then, in 1755, an Act was obtained to make the Sankey Brook, from the Mersey to St Helens, navigable. Instead of simply improving the existing channel, however, the engineer, Henry Berry, determined to make an artificial waterway—a canal, later known as the St Helens Canal. Four years later, in 1759, came the Act for the first major undertaking of the canal age. In 1761 the Bridgewater Canal was opened from the mines at Worsley to Manchester. The figures for 1898 show a grand total of 4,012 miles of canal and river navigation in England, Scotland and Wales; to that can be added a further 540 miles of derelict navigations. It is fair, then, to say that at the system's greatest extent there were over four and a half thousand miles of navigable waterways in Great Britain.

As the canal system developed, some of the engineers began to regard river navigations as obsolete. James Brindley considered that rivers 'were made to feed canals', and proposed improving the navigation above Battersea by substituting a canal for the Thames. But in practice river and canal navigations were interdependent; twelve canals connected with the Severn and its estuary and six canals with the Thames. River navigations had some advantages, as the engineer William Jessop pointed out; they were cheaper to construct and maintain, and they were wider, with fewer bridges, thus enabling sailing vessels to be used without the continuous necessity of horse-towing. They were also cheaper to use; Zachary Allnutt, a superintendent on the Thames in the early nineteenth century, quotes the carriage rates of goods per ton-mile on the rivers as ranging between 1¾d (½p) and 3¼d (1½p), whereas on the canals the range was between 3¾d and 6d (2½p). He notes that in usual conditions it took between five and six days for a barge to complete the voyage on the Thames between Lechlade and London, a distance of 146 miles, while it took a whole day to travel the 8 miles of the Stroudwater Canal, a particularly slow waterway owing to the number of locks and the absence of continuous towing-paths. On the Trent, according to Jessop, a double journey of 140 miles was often completed in a week, including the time taken for loading and unloading.

With the development of the railways, the canals began to lose their commercial attraction; capital invested in them was diverted to railway companies which themselves bought a large number of canals, building their lines on some and allowing others to deteriorate over the years. Trade on many rivers, however, increased with the connection of their ports to the railway network, especially on the lower reaches and estuaries. The Thames, Tyne, Trent, Forth and Clyde are among the major rivers of England and Scotland which are still commercially important.

Let us look in more detail at the history of some of the navigations. The Severn, as we have seen, was said in the reign of Henry VII to have been a navigation since 'time out of mind'. This certainly goes back to the days of Roman colonisation, when there was a quay at Gloucester, about thirty yards east of the present quay, on a channel of the river that has since changed its course. Some centuries later a charter of Henry II, dating from the middle of the twelfth century, commanded that 'the men of Gloucester and all those who wish to go by the River Severn shall have their way and passage by the Severn with wood and coals and timber and all their merchandises freely and quietly, and we forbid

Navigation on the Severn at Gloucester, from an engraving by
J. Walker, 1793

anyone from vexing or disturbing them in aught hereupon'. The
importance to medieval Gloucester of river-borne trade can be deduced
by the effect on the city of the development of the port of Bristol in the
fourteenth and fifteenth centuries, when it was stated in a petition to
Henry VII that 300 dwellings had fallen into decay and Gloucester as a
whole was in a state of ruin and desolation. Above Gloucester,
Tewkesbury, Worcester, Bewdley, Bridgnorth and Shrewsbury all
developed into inland ports. Except for Bewdley, all these towns are
marked on Gough's map of Great Britain made in 1360; Bewdley's
development was rather later and from here in the fifteenth century
firewood was shipped down to Worcester and Gloucester.

By the reign of Elizabeth, coal was being mined alongside the banks
of the Severn and was transported to the cathedral cities by boat. Some
idea of the variety of goods carried along the river can be gained from
the Port Books of Bristol; Shrewsbury and Bridgnorth sent mainly wool,
Bewdley leather, skins, wax, honey and staves for barrels, and Worcester
wool and manufactured cloth. Up river from Bristol came wine, soap,
iron, lead, oil, rosin, liquorice, oranges, dye-wood, alum, groceries,

canvas and linens. Then, with the industrial developments in the upper Severn valley as we move into the seventeenth century, a change becomes apparent; more manufactured goods, including scythes, nails, paper and brass pots, are carried downriver while raw materials figure largely in the cargoes from Bristol. Water transport was generally quick and always cheap, for longer journeys perhaps only one-tenth of the cost of transport by road. Early Acts of Parliament attempted to ensure that the Severn was an entirely free river, but the riverside towns fought a long and eventually successful battle for the right to charge tolls on goods landed at their quays. Their attempts, however, to intercept boats in transit and force the boatmen to sell their cargoes there and then or charge them merely for the privilege of passing by were abandoned before the end of the sixteenth century.

While the towns and inland ports of the Severn valley continued to prosper, there seems to have been no attempt made to improve the condition of the navigation. 'There is no river that has such a length of navigation as the Severn,' wrote Richard Whitworth in 1766. 'You may navigate a vessel of 50 tons, and not a lock the whole way, 200 miles up to Welshpool, except in an excessive drought.' About this time, the boats mainly used on the river were of two kinds: barges, 40-60ft in length, with a single mast and square sail, carrying from 20-40 tons, and trows, carrying 40-80 tons, with a square sail and a top sail on the mainmast, some of them also with a mizzen mast carrying a lateen sail. In earlier years the boats were smaller; none of the Worcester boats recorded in the sixteenth century was valued at more than £10, and a trow built in 1657 to carry timber could carry only 20 tons. Other Severn craft, in later years, included narrow boats off some of the canals—the Staffordshire & Worcestershire, Worcester & Birmingham, Droitwich, Hereford & Gloucester and Gloucester & Berkeley—that connected with the river. When the Thames & Severn Canal was opened in 1789, trows could navigate via the Stroudwater Canal to Brimscombe where goods were transhipped into barges for the rest of the journey. In 1800 a barge completed the through passage from Coalbrookdale to London in two weeks.

The canals brought a great increase of traffic on the Severn, and not only those canals that connected directly with it. Towards the end of the eighteenth century the Shropshire tub-boat canal network was developed to serve the ironworks and coalfield of East Shropshire. For two centuries before this time, coal had been a major cargo, being carried upwards to mid-Wales as well as downriver. Likewise Broseley-clay tobacco pipes and pottery mugs from Jackfield were distributed by river craft. It was the Shropshire coalfield that fed the developing iron industry; there were notable concentrations of forges in the valleys of two Severn tributaries, the Tern and the Worfe; the lower stretch of the Tern was navigable in the early eighteenth century. The rapid expansion of the iron industry, following the taking over of the Coalbrookdale works by Abraham Darby I in 1708, where he introduced coke smelting, led to greater use of the river. But as the demands on the river increased, so its condition as a navigation deteriorated. Towards the end of the eighteenth century the water level in summer was frequently too low to permit the passage of loaded boats; in 1796 the river in Shropshire was usable for only eight weeks altogether. The Severn was a free river; the vessels using it were either individually owned or in only small fleets, and the owners showed no concern in improving the navigation themselves. The ironmasters, who controlled so much else, were never able to take over the barge traffic, and the canal companies, who wanted the river improved, could not overcome the opposition of the barge-owners. Until William Reynolds, one of the great ironmasters, built a length of towpath suitable for use by horses at his own cost, haulage of boats was by manpower. This towpath was extended by stages until by 1812 it reached from Shrewsbury to Gloucester. Reynolds was also greatly involved in the Shropshire tub-boat canals and developed a canal-river interchange at Coalport, where coal and other heavy goods were offloaded from the tub-boats and carried by inclined railways to the riverside. These wharves and the basin at Coalport have recently been excavated by the Ironbridge Gorge Museum Trust, which has recalled and restored so much of the industrial past of this area.

Shortage of water in the summer was one problem; the condition of the Severn estuary was another. Between Sharpness and Gloucester larger vessels could only use the river at spring tides; shifting sandbanks and rapid floods—not to mention the Bore—caused great dangers. To avoid the most troublesome part of the estuary the Gloucester & Berkeley Ship Canal was authorised in 1793; when it was opened—not until 1827—it immediately improved the situation both below and above Gloucester. The next decade or so heard much debate about improvements to the river between Gloucester and Stourport, with the various canal companies and other interested parties failing to agree on the details of what should be done. In 1842 the Severn Improvement Association was formed with the support of the powerful Staffs & Worcs Canal Co, several industrial companies and the merchants of Gloucester and Worcester. About this time James Walker, reporting for the Gloucester & Berkeley Canal Company, counted about 3,400 canal boats, 549 trows and 405 barges using the Severn above Gloucester. A commission was set up to improve the river from Gloucester to the Gladder Brook just above Stourport by the construction of locks and by dredging. Work was completed by the end of 1846, five locks having been built and the channel dredged, according to the chief engineer William Cubitt, to minimum depth of 6ft, at an approximate cost of £180,000. Tolls for the first year mounted to over £11,000, collected on 450,000 tons of goods. But it was found that the 6ft depth could not be maintained, and toll receipts began to fall. In 1853 the commissioners obtained an Act enabling them to liquidate their debts and to have another lock built at Tewkesbury. Soon steam tugs began to appear on the river and as the years passed the number of horse-drawn craft diminished and the towpath companies' receipts dwindled away. With the increase of railways the upper river became less used; 1862 saw the last traffic above Shrewsbury and 1895 the end of trade to Bridgnorth. Stourport became the head of navigation. Below Stourport trade also decreased, until the building of oil storage wharves near Worcester in the late 1920s. This brought a revival in the fortunes of the Severn for a time; trade in oil, timber, grain, aluminium and other commodities continued until well into the 1960s, at times exceeding ¾ million tons a year. Then the oil wharves at Worcester and Stourport were closed and trading above Gloucester came virtually to an end. Between Gloucester and Stourport the river is used increasingly by pleasure cruisers but as a commercial highway it is sadly no longer of any significance.

Before the age of canals, the Severn was the greatest of England's trading rivers; indeed, it was once described as the second busiest river in Europe. Yet very little parliamentary activity was devoted to the Severn, bearing in mind its commercial importance. The Thames, by comparison, has been dealt with in a multitude of Acts, as well as being the first river to come under the control of a single conservancy authority for the whole of its length. The Thames is also by far the best documented and most frequently illustrated of our rivers.

The Thames and Severn shared one distinction, that of being able to carry larger vessels further inland than any other rivers in Britain. Another distinction belongs to the Thames alone: it is the country's greatest recreational waterway. The turning point in the relative value between commerce and recreation occurred in the 1880s, when the tolls taken on the non-tidal river above Teddington from pleasure craft overtook the receipts from commercial barge traffic. Rowing, by this time, had been a regular river activity for about fifty years, but the rapid development of the Thames pleasure boatyards seems to have coincided

A comparatively modest mid-Victorian houseboat, from Mr and Mrs Hall's *Book of the Thames*, 1859

with the offers of cheap rail excursion tickets to riverside resorts. In 1883 an Act was passed enabling the Thames Conservancy to charge fees for steam launches using the river, and two years later a further Act extended registration to cover all pleasure craft from houseboats to canoes. By this time the river's major regatta, Henley, established in 1839, had become 'a society show'. 'Again the bustle, the excitement, the heart-burnings, the petty squabbles, the troops of brown legged savages in blood-red blazers, the niggers, the rattle of oars—what a wonderful thing is Henley!' wrote a correspondent in 1888. The *Illustrated London News* described the regatta as 'one of the most delightful entertainments of the season', and *Punch*, in its hints for visitors, recommended that 'if you really wish to make a favourable impression upon everyone, be cheery, contented, good-natured, and, above all, slightly interested in the racing'. Contemporary illustrations show the river at Henley so crowded that it looks possible to cross from bank to bank without getting one's feet wet. There were other regattas too, at Richmond, Datchet and Sunbury, with fêtes, fireworks and girls who appeared 'to be sent straight from paradise'. Apart from the boats used for racing, there were gigs and skiffs, punts, canoes, steam launches—generally unpopular except with those actually aboard them—and those peculiarly Victorian craft, the houseboats.

Houseboats originated as passenger-carrying barges, horse-drawn, the passengers being able either to enjoy the view from the 'room' or the fresh air from the deck. In the room were seats and a table, and the whole thing was gaily painted. With the coming of the steam tug the houseboats increased in size and elaboration; the wealthy commissioned their own, taking them to the more fashionable regattas. In *Victorians on the Thames*, R.S. Bolland describes some of the splendid houseboats with their floral decorations, fairy lights, saloons, kitchens, bedrooms and wine cellars. Two of the largest were owned by Mr Henry Hewett: the *Kingfisher*, too big to pass through the locks above Molesey, and the *Satsuma*, which could be taken apart and floated through the locks in two halves. The main saloon of the *Satsuma* was 750 square feet and the deck saloon 850 square feet, with thirty-two pairs of windows. The vessel was full of Satsuma vases of all shapes and sizes and was furnished in rich Victorian style. When Mr Hewett sold her, the advertisement read: 'First floor dining saloon accommodating 200 persons, seven bedrooms, kitchen, winecellar, etc. Second floor immense dancing saloon, a promenade terrace. Third deck bunting, rigging, etc.' He never allowed smoking on board, in case of fire; after he sold her, she did catch fire and was totally destroyed. Since the days of the *Satsuma*, the number of houseboats on the Thames has, apart from the late 1930s and the 1940s, fluctuated little; in 1909 there were 160 and in 1975 there were 205. In that same period, while the number of small craft remained stable, launches increased from 861 to 15,869. Some idea of the present use of the river by pleasure craft can be gained from the fact that, yearly, more than one million passages are made through the locks.

Until the late 1930s, the picturesque sailing barges were the characteristic craft of the tidal Thames, the Medway and some of the eastern tidal rivers. The Medway was navigable to Maidstone in the sixteenth century; it was improved up to Tonbridge about 1750, when several locks were built and further improved below Maidstone some fifty years later. Maidstone and Rochester became barge-building centres. In 1798 the river was described as carrying 'a considerable traffic', including the manufactures of the many fulling- and paper-mills and 'vast quantities of timber brought hither from the Weald of Kent'. Barges known as 'stumpies' were developed for river work; they had no topmast and their beam was restricted to about 14ft so that they could negotiate the various bridges. Among other cargoes they carried refuse from London rubbish dumps to the brickyards of Kent, returning loaded with bricks. Edgar March describes the river as it must have looked about 1874, when it was still a busy navigation: 'The Medway was alive with sailing craft; dainty little topsail schooners, picturesque collier brigs with apple bows and dingy canvas, barques from Scandinavia, bringing pine-scented timber from the Baltic to Rochester, and, above all, barges innumerable, threading their way through a maze of traffic. One hundred a tide was no uncommon sight, and what a joy to a sail-lover that galaxy of russet, brown and ochre canvas must have been, many with various devices emblazoned on their mainsails—Lee's stumpies had the white horse of Kent rampant on ebony-coloured sails—all either hurrying down on the ebb or beating up against wind and tide. Now gone for ever.'

In later years barges were much used in the cement trade; the Associated Portland Cement Manufacturers ran a fleet of 282 barges earlier this century. Stackies—hay and straw barges—were built rather wider and more shallow for their special cargoes. Root crops or corn would be loaded into the hold and the hay stacked on deck, often carried to London to feed the hundreds of thousands of horses before the age of the motor car. Some of the Essex barges were steered by lines from the tiller operated by a man standing on top of the stack—he could even see where he was going, an undoubted advantage. Stackies were convenient for smuggling; contraband from foreign ships could be transferred in the Thames estuary and the barge then proceeded innocently upriver. Smuggled goods were sometimes shifted from barges into canal boats and so right into the Midlands. But the penalties if you were caught were tough; the barge would be seized and sawn in two and its skipper pressed into the Navy for a period of some years as a punishment.

The Thames and Severn—although not the Medway—are two of the 'first-class' rivers in the classification we have already referred to. The others in this list are the Humber, Mersey, Yorkshire Ouse, Great Ouse, Trent, Witham and Wye. Of these, the Wye is the least important as a navigation, whether for trade or pleasure; it may be possible to get up as far as Tintern, but above there the river is of use only for rowing or canoeing. The Wye was navigable by small craft in the Tudor period; it was improved in the mid-seventeenth century when flash-locks were installed and at some time boats could sail as far as Hay. Its tributary, the Lugg, was also navigable for a time up to Leominster, according to Defoe who comments on the trade in corn and wool from that town via Lugg, Wye and Severn to Bristol. Defoe also mentions the good trade of Ross on the River Wye. Small trows were used on the Wye, having to be hauled by men when conditions demanded except for the stretch between Hereford and Lydbrook where a towing path was constructed in 1811. Between 1830 and 1860 there were passenger services on the river from Chepstow to Ross, but by the end of this period there was little commercial carrying and before 1900 all had finished.

The Witham has a far longer history as a navigation than most of the other major rivers, but it can hardly be said to have been crowded with incident. The river itself was improved by the Romans, who also cut the Fossdyke to make a continuous waterway from the Wash at Boston to the Trent. Lincoln, at the junction of Fossdyke and Witham, was also served by the Car Dyke which connected the city to the Cambridgeshire waterways. In the centuries after the Romans left, while the Fossdyke was on occasions cleansed and improved, the Witham ceased to be navigable, serving only for drainage purposes. It did not recover until the second half of the eighteenth century; under an Act of 1762 the sluice at Boston was rebuilt as the Grand Sluice, with a lock for navigation alongside it, and three more locks were constructed on the river. Some forty-five years later, replacements and improvements were put in hand under a scheme proposed by John Rennie. The Witham Navigation was moderately busy in the following decades, although toll receipts show that the Fossdyke was more prosperous than the river. Steam packets appeared in 1816, competing first with the sailing vessels, which they defeated, and then in the years following 1848 with the Great Northern Railway, whose line from Boston to Lincoln ran along the river bank. The navigation had in fact been leased to the railway, which had to maintain it although all the passenger and most of the freight traffic soon deserted the water. Today the Witham, and some of its connecting navigable drains, is used by pleasure cruisers; Brayford Pool in Lincoln is busy, but most of the craft there go to and from the Trent. The Glory-hole at Lincoln is one of the better known waterway sights; Boston Stump, at the mouth of the river, is another.

The Great Ouse and its tributaries also have a long navigational history. As well as the Car Dyke, most of the Cambridgeshire lodes—manmade rivers flowing into the Cam—date from the Roman occupation; the Romans used the water route to convey grain and hides to their garrisons in the north. As highways the Fenland rivers, until comparatively recent times, have always been very important. Writing in 1722, Defoe described Lynn as having 'the greatest extent of inland navigation of any port in England, London excepted. The reason whereof is this,' he continued, 'that there are more navigable rivers empty themselves here into the sea . . . than at any one mouth of waters in England, except the Thames and the Humber. By these navigable rivers the merchants of Lynn supply about six counties wholly, and three counties in part, with their goods, especially wine and coals, which has

Lithograph of King's Lynn, about 1840. Note the gang of lighters in the right foreground

given rise to this observation on the town of Lynn, that they bring in more coals, than any sea-port between London and Bristol.' Long before the time of Defoe, stone for the building of the major religious foundations at Ely and Bury St Edmunds was carried by water from the quarries at Barnack. Until the building of the first Denver Sluice in 1652 boats could be sailed into the upper reaches of the Fen rivers. Because the Sluice limited the size of vessels, the Fen lighter was developed as a purpose-built craft for these waterways. Lighters operated in gangs, hauled by a horse and later by steam tugs; being of shallow draught they could penetrate the whole system of rivers and navigable drains. Until World War II, roads were few and far between in the Fenland, but there were several rail-waterway interchange basins, and villages and farms were adequately served by lighters and barges. Many of the pumping stations on which the security of the area depended received their supplies of fuel by water; coal came on the lighters and, later, oil was distributed by Appleyard's tanker *Shellfen*. By the early 1960s commercial traffic was finished, however, and the lighters gave way to the smart pleasure cruisers.

On the upper river, the navigation reached Bedford in 1689. At its greatest, the Ouse network extended to Bedford, Cambridge, Shefford (on the Ivel navigation, 1823), Bury St Edmunds (on the Lark), Thetford (on the Little Ouse), Northwold (on the Wissey), and above Narborough (on the Nar), in addition to the villages at the heads of the lodes—Bottisham, Swaffham, Reach, Burwell, Wicken and Soham. There has been some contraction; Bedford was inaccessible from early on in this century until 1978, the Ivel Navigation ceased in 1876, the upper Lark was unnavigable by about 1850 and commercial traffic on the Little Ouse had stopped by 1914, the upper 9 miles of the river now being unusable except by canoes. Only a mile or so of the Wissey has been lost, but navigation on the Nar ended in 1884. Swaffham, Reach and Burwell lodes are still open to pleasure craft. On the other side of the Great Ouse it is still possible to voyage by various routes through the artificial rivers of the Middle Level to reach the Nene at Stanground, below Peterborough.

Before the thirteenth century, the Great Ouse and the Nene made a common outfall into the Wash in the vicinity of Wisbech. Since then both nature and man have had their effect on these rivers. Part of a southern branch of the Nene as it was has been incorporated into the navigations of the Middle Level; the main channel of the old river has vanished altogether and the Nene from Peterborough to the Wash is artificial. While Wisbech has been—and still is—of some importance as a port, now some 11½ miles from the outfall, the history of the navigation of the river as a whole is a rather miserable one. Bits of the river were navigable by small craft before the legislation of the eighteenth century, but the many mills with their associated dams and weirs, and a number of long, low bridges made passage difficult. The Nene is the sixth longest river in England; Northampton is 91 miles from the Wash. Work on making the river properly navigable began in 1726; 35 years later, the first barges reached Northampton, laden with coal. In 1815, after lengthy negotiations, the river navigation was linked to the canal system by the Northampton arm of the Grand Junction Canal. Trade on the river, however, never came up to expectations; floods were frequent, there were thirty-four locks and eleven difficult and dangerous staunches, the course of the river through Wisbech was often obstructed and the outfall was inadequate. The new Outfall Cut, completed in 1824, solved one problem, but despite the expenditure of nearly £200,000 in the mid-nineteenth century on the river below Peterborough its condition continued to deteriorate. At last in the 1930s, the Nene Catchment Board removed the staunches, rebuilt the locks, and greatly improved the quay and the course of the

Wisbech & Ely

UNION

Packet Boat

Edward Stevens, *Owner*, John Lee, *Master.*

THE Public are most respectfully informed that the above Boat leaves Wisbech every Monday Morning, at Seven o'Clock, from the Canal Sluice, for the Conveyance of Goods and Passengers through Elm, Emneth, Outwell, Nordelph, Salter's Lode, Denver Sluice, Littleport, to Ely, where it arrives the same Afternoon; whence Goods may be quickly forwarded to Soham, Fordham, Downham in the Isle, Stretham, Milton, Waterbeach, Wilburton, Haddenham, Witchford, Witcham, Coveney, Sutton, Mepal, Cambridge, Newmarket, Bury, and all other places adjacent. The Packet Boat will leave Ely every Friday Morning, at Eight o'Clock, from the New Quay, and arrive at Wisbech the same Afternoon, when Goods may be forwarded the following day, to Guyhirn, Wisbech St. Mary's, Parson Drove, Leverington, Newton, Tydd St. Giles, Tydd St. Mary's, Sutton St. Edmund's, Long Sutton, Gedney, Fleet, Holbeach, Spalding, Boston, March, Chatteris, &c.

The greatest care will be taken of the Goods entrusted to the Master, and the delivery punctually attended to.

☞ Small Parcels may be left to the care of Mr. W. STEVENS, Draper, York Row, Wisbech.

Wisbech, 12th July, 1831.

(*H. & J. Leach, Printers, Wisbech.*

From Wisbech on the Nene to Ely on the Great Ouse, 1831

river through Wisbech. Narrow boats resumed carrying imported wheat to Whitworth's at Wellingborough after the war and a few sailing barges traded to Peterborough, but by 1970 all commercial traffic ceased, except for the transport of stone from Wansford to line the banks of the lower river. Like the Great Ouse, but not to the same extent, the Nene is now the resort of pleasure cruisers.

All the remaining 'first-class' rivers still carry commercial traffic. Into the Humber estuary flow all the navigable rivers of Yorkshire, as well as the River Trent. The Romans conveyed supplies up the Ouse to York, and current excavations in the city are adding greatly to our knowledge of the extent of the trade during the Viking occupation. In the middle ages York was a very prosperous inland port. Above the city navigation was carried on to Boroughbridge on the Ure, on the Swale and on the Foss. Below York, the Wharfe and Derwent were also navigable. In south Yorkshire the Don was open to Doncaster and the Idle, a tributary of the Trent, to Bawtry. Another navigable river was the Hull, as far up as Wansford, with a connection to Beverley via the short Beverley Beck. With the increase in size of sea-going vessels, however, the long voyages up winding rivers became less appealing. Overseas traders came to prefer the more convenient port of Kingston-upon-Hull, and, as Hull grew, the importance of York and Beverley declined. By the end of the fifteenth century most of the Yorkshire rivers were markedly less used than they had been a hundred years before. Under the Tudors, York was still busy with small craft plying to and from Hull, but had no ships or mariners of its own. In 1565 the Ouse Bridge collapsed, which helped neither trade nor local morale. Despite silting, the river continued to be navigable, though not always with ease. Several attempts were made to obtain legislation and to raise money for river improvements but it was a long time before anything really significant happened. The construction of Naburn lock and weir in 1757 improved the upper river but caused shoals to develop below it. Mention of a few dates, however, will give a picture of what was happening elsewhere in Yorkshire in the eighteenth century. In 1704 the Aire & Calder Navigation was opened, first to Castleford and then to Leeds and Wakefield. The Calder & Hebble extended navigation from Wakefield to Sowerby Bridge in 1770, and Sir John Ramsden's canal linked Huddersfield to the Calder & Hebble in 1776. The Selby Canal, joining Selby to the Aire & Calder, opened in 1778. The movement was to west and south Yorkshire, to Leeds, Bradford, Halifax, Huddersfield, Barnsley, Rotherham and Sheffield, all eventually served by water transport with connections to the far side of the Pennines through the Leeds & Liverpool, Rochdale and

Huddersfield Narrow canals. A canal was opened from Goole to Ferrybridge in 1826 and in the next year Goole became a port with its own customs facilities and took over much of the traffic from Selby. On the Ouse itself improvements were made above York, with the Linton Lock Navigation and Ripon Canal both being opened by 1772 and the Foss improved some years later. This brought more business to York, but the Ouse could no longer be regarded as a major navigation. Not even the making of the Cod Beck navigable from the Swale to Thirsk was enough; only two cargo-carrying boats are recorded as having made the voyage from Thirsk to York, despite the firing of 'patteraroes' that greeted the passing of the Cod Beck Navigation Act.

Almost all the Yorkshire waterways were worked by the Humber

Keels on opposite tacks, on the Trent in the early 1920s

keels, craft that in essentials seem to have descended from the Vikings and are not dissimilar to the troop-carriers of William of Normandy. The keel was characterised by its tall, forward-set, single mast with a large square sail; on later and larger keels a topsail could be set as well, to catch the wind above tree-top height. As on the Norfolk wherries, the mast could be lowered to pass under bridges. Keels were up to 60ft long and 15ft beam; a large example could carry up to 100 tons. They were bluff-bowed and flat-bottomed and were often fitted with leeboards to prevent drifting. A crew of two—often a man and boy—was sufficient to work a keel. They survived well into the twentieth century, the *Nar* still sailing in 1949.

Larger than the keels were the Humber sloops, with fore-and-aft rig and a triangular foresail but similar-shaped hull. Sloops were developed in the eighteenth century and were used on the wider rivers and for coastal trade to and from the Wash, London and the south-coast ports. They needed more room to manoeuvre than keels and so were less suitable for canals and the upper reaches of rivers, but they were faster and could carry up to about 150 tons. Sadly no wooden-hulled keel or sloop has been preserved, but the steel-hulled *Comrade* is being revitalised and re-rigged by the Humber Keel & Sloop Preservation 'society, in much the same way as the wherry *Albion* has been saved by the Norfolk Wherry Trust. Motor-powered keels and barges still use the Yorkshire waterways, and, in the past, variants of the keel were used on the Tyne, the Norfolk Broads and the Teign in Devon.

The first steamboat appeared on the Yorkshire Ouse in 1816. Within two decades a flourishing passenger service developed between York and London; three steamers, the *Arrow*, *Ebor* and *Old Ebor*, sailed regularly from York to connect at Hull with the *Vivid*, *Wilberforce* and *Waterwitch* for London. A saloon cost 11s (55p) and a fore-cabin 7s (35p). The York steamers also connected with the railway. This service ended by 1875, but a few years later a local steamer passenger service was operating between York and several riverside villages. Nowadays only one or two commercial vessels a week reach York, though the staithes and warehouses are constant reminders of the old trading story of the city.

The Trent is the third longest of English rivers and was navigable from Nottingham to the Humber in early times. Gainsborough was a major river port by the mid-seventeenth century; goods to and from Nottingham were transhipped there as the river between those towns was too shallow for sea-going craft. Attempts to make the river above Nottingham navigable met with fierce opposition from the traders of

The Ouse Bridge at York, 1828

Nottingham itself and of the other ports on the lower river, who wanted to keep as much business as possible in their own hands. An Act to make the river navigable to Burton-on-Trent was obtained in 1699, but by this time Wilden Ferry, a short distance above the confluence with the Derwent, was in effect the head of navigation and a large trade, particularly in cheese, had been built up. Burton became a river port in 1712 and a whole variety of goods passed along the upper Trent for almost a hundred years, until the opening of the Trent & Mersey Canal, which locked into the river at Shardlow. Shardlow now developed as a port, and by the early 1800s the river above was hardly used.

The importance of the Trent in the canal age can be seen from the number of canals that connected with it. In addition to the Trent & Mersey, the Derby, Nottingham, Grantham, Erewash and Chesterfield canals locked into the river; there was also a connection with the Grand Junction (later the Grand Union) via the Leicester and Loughborough navigations. At the beginning of the nineteenth century there were about 140 barges using the river; a steam packet began regular passenger service between Nottingham and Gainsborough in 1817 and Gainsborough obtained customs facilities in 1841. The Trent Navigation Co was making comfortable profits and rejected suggestions that the river be improved to take larger vessels. The river, therefore, was not prepared for railway competition; the company was forced to reduce tolls to retain traffic and a long battle for survival began. Many of the connecting canals were bought by railways and allowed to run down. Nevertheless, by the beginning of the present century the river was carrying up to 400,000 tons a year; it was dredged, new locks were built and a profitable traffic in petroleum began in 1913. Since then the fortunes of the navigation have continued to fluctuate. Recently a regular direct service between Gainsborough and Rotterdam has begun and cargoes are still carried to Nottingham. But many of the large riverside warehouses no longer serve riverborne trade; too many lorries thunder along the roads of the east Midlands while the river flows idly along.

The two remaining 'first-class' rivers, the Tyne and the Mersey, are tidal navigations only. The Tyne is navigable for 19 miles, and is used almost entirely by sea-going vessels. The Mersey is navigable to Warrington; it also connects with the Manchester Ship Canal and with the Weaver which takes sea-going ships from Weston Point to the ICI works below the Anderton lift. The Mersey and the Weaver had their own particular type of craft, the flats, sailing barges up to 68ft long and 16ft wide, which dominated the scene during the eighteenth and

'Frendo Norden', Gainsborough Line, on the Trent near Gains-
borough. This 700-tonne vessel was specially designed to operate on
British and mainland European inland waterways. The service between
Gainsborough and Rotterdam started in 1976

nineteenth centuries until they yielded to the steam barges, towing
trains of dumb barges. The river flats had masts that could be lowered,
like those of the keels and Norfolk wherries, but the coastal flats had
fixed masts. Both the Bridgewater and Rochdale canals were constructed
to take flats.

A map of the watersheds and inland navigations of the United
Kingdom, published in 1906, shows fifty-two. river navigations in
England and Wales and five in Scotland. Many of them are now disused
or navigable only in part, or by canoes or very light craft. All of them in
their time carried goods but it is not easy to ascertain the extent of
regular passenger carriage. Several of the early Navigation Acts refer to
passengers and sometimes tolls or fares are stipulated, but evidence of
numbers of people carried or the regularity of services is hard to come by.
For the most part it seems that people took a boat when they needed to;
Defoe, for example, 'having a mind to view the harbour', sent his
horses round by Manningtree and 'took a boat up the River Orwell for
Ipswich', a voyage of 12 miles from Harwich. In the Fens, particularly in
medieval times, matters were rather different; in the absence of any
alternatives, the waterways were used for the carriage of both goods and
people. 'From the frequent mention of boats and boat-hire it would

seem that the ordinary "sewers" were the highways from place to place', writes H. C. Darby in *The Medieval Fenland*, and he quotes several examples from the Witham southwards to the Great Ouse and the lodes. Part of a tenant's duty was often to provide a boat and boatman for his lord, and the sacrist of Ely and his companions travelled around the diocese by boat. Nor was royal water travel confined to the Thames; about 1300 a fleet of thirty-seven barges and boats conveyed the king and his court from Boston to Lincoln along the Witham. Today the bishops of Ely and Huntingdon still tour their dioceses by boat.

Navigating rivers for pleasure was very much a development of the Victorian age. No fewer than fifty-five boat-builders and hirers operating between Putney and Oxford advertised in Taunt's *Map of the Thames* published about 1880. Jerome K. Jerome's *Three Men in a Boat*, published in 1890, is only the best-known of many accounts of pleasure boating. It is worth remembering that the Victorian pleasure-seekers either rowed or punted in small boats, or massed together in large companies on river steamers. The Thames was the most

Coal on the Humber

The first of the Clyde paddle-steamers. From an aquatint by William Daniell, published 1817

popular river for pleasure, but not the only one; there were many pleasure steamers on the Forth and Clyde, and the *Pride of the Ouse* carried twenty passengers on tours of the Fen waterways from Thetford.

The Clyde needs more than a passing mention. The first steamer on the river, the *Comet*, went into service in 1812 between Glasgow and Helensburgh, on the north side of the Firth. In the 1830s there were nearly forty vessels steaming from Broomielaw, in the centre of Glasgow, to Campbeltown, Ayr and other western ports. Famous steamers in the late Victorian years included the *Columba*, built 1878, flagship of the MacBrayne fleet and completed to the highest standards of luxury, the *Lord of the Isles*, owned by the Glasgow & Inveraray Steamship Company and sailing between those two ports, and the *Ivanhoe*. This last was unique in that she was teetotal, a successful attempt to prove that it was possible to enjoy a voyage on a steamer without recourse to alcohol. She became very popular with middle-class Glaswegians—or at least with their wives and children—and, skippered by James Williamson, who became manager of the Firth of Clyde Steam Packet Company, she was always a clean and tidy ship. Between 1889 and 1914 there were seventy-five paddle steamers on the Clyde, many owned by competing railway companies. Some of them survived the war, including *Columba*, broken up in 1936, and a handful lasted into the 1940s, with *Queen Alexandra II* paddling on until 1958.

Another, and very different, river much used by paddle steamers was the Tamar. Regular service began here in the 1820s between Plymouth, Calstock and Weir Head, near Gunnislake. As the population of Plymouth and Devonport grew, so the steamer service became more popular until in 1856 the Queen, Prince Albert and their children sailed up to Morwellham in the steamer *Gipsy*. This brought added publicity to the Tamar and its steamers, and more trippers disembarked at Calstock to visit its beer-houses. In 1865 a Clyde-built steamer, *Ariel*, came to the Tamar, setting a new standard of luxury with separate lavatories for men and women. Then came *Eleanor*, *Empress* and *Alexandra*; between 1865 and 1914 there were seventeen paddle steamers on the river. *Empress* was the last survivor, succeeded by the diesel powered *Devon Belle* in 1935.

Restoration of the old port of Morwellham has been in progress for the past few years and you can take a boat trip from Plymouth to see the old copper quays, the lime kilns, wharf cottages and exhibits to do with nineteenth-century mining. At one time, Morwellham was the port for Tavistock; in 1238 it was handling sea-sand, for fertilising the fields, cider and dried fish, and exported tin from Dartmoor. In the industrial age the Devon Great Consols mine near Tavistock, which had thirty-three wheels operated by water raised from the Tamar, and the mines of Wheal Betsy, Wheal Friendship, Wheal Crebor and others, exported their output of copper, arsenic, manganese and lead through Morwellham. In 1817 the Tavistock Canal, with its long tunnel through Morwell Down, was opened, connecting with Morwellham on the river below by means of an inclined plane falling 237ft. But in the second half of the century the mines began to fail and the railways moved in to take off what trade there was. The port fell into disuse; in 1896 'not a ship was on the river' a visitor said. Ten years ago it was described as a 'ghost village, lost amid a desolation of weed and ooze'. Since then it has been taken in hand by the Dartington Amenity Research Trust and much has been restored. And on the other bank of the Tamar the National Maritime Museum has mounted displays on the history of the Tamar. *Shamrock*, the last barge to work on the river, has been restored and is moored at the quayside there.

View from the Foundry Bridge, Norwich, by James Stark, 1834

After the Thames and Clyde, however, perhaps the waterways most used for pleasure as well as for goods and passenger carrying were—and are—the Norfolk Broads. For centuries Yarmouth was a major port in European trade. In 1656 Francis Matthew, one of the pioneers of improvements in inland navigation, proposed making a link between the Waveney and the Little Ouse, which rise within about a mile of each other, and improving the Fossdyke, so that connection could be made between Yarmouth and York 'to the unspeakable comfort of many towns and villages lying near or upon the Passage'. Although nearly all goods to Yarmouth had to be transhipped there for the journey up the Yare to Norwich, as the river was suitable only for shallow draught vessels, Norwich became a trading centre nearly as important as Bristol. Over 600 trading wherries were built.

Passenger-carrying on the Yare developed early, there being references to it from the fourteenth century onwards. The vessels used were generally described as 'barges', and they usually seem to have been rowed. In the mid-seventeenth century the fare from Norwich to Yarmouth was 6d (2½p), and from Beccles to Yarmouth 4d (2p). The first steam packet appeared in 1813 to be followed by several more. The boiler of one of them, the *Telegraph*, exploded in 1817 and half the twenty-two people on board were killed. For a time this made passengers wary of steamers, and the owner of the *Courier*, the *Telegraph*'s sister ship, converted the vessel into a horse packet, with four horses walking around a shaft in the hold to provide power to drive the paddlewheels. The steamers soon regained their popularity, however, and retained it throughout the nineteenth century, although, with the coming of railways, their owners turned from the regular carriage of passengers to the hiring of their vessels as trip-boats.

Early in that century the Broads became the great water-playground that they still are. 'Annually in July the Mayors of Norwich and Yarmouth meet in their state barges on the river Yare', wrote William Taylor. 'All the many pleasure boats kept on these rivers assemble; the commercial craft is in requisition to stow spectators, to waft music, to vend refreshments: such of the shipping as ascends above the Yarmouth drawbridge, is moored within ken; there are sailing matches, rowing matches, and spontaneous evolutions of vessels of all sorts, a dance of ships, their streamers flying and their canvas spread. It is a fair afloat, where the voice of revelry resounds from every gliding tent.' There were Water Frolics at Beccles, Burgh, Wroxham, Hickling—throughout the Broads, in fact, with wherry races becoming an important feature of them in the second half of the century. It was then that the first pleasure wherries appeared, at first converted from trading wherries but later purpose built to carry passengers, often luxuriously fitted out with a piano on board. The last of the pleasure wherries—more than 70 were launched—was built about fifty years ago. *Albion* is now the only wherry under sail; there are a few converted wherry hulls still to be seen, but motor cruisers, yachts and dinghies have predominated on the Broads for several decades.

Our rivers have served as highways for two thousand years and more. Except for their estuaries, very few of them are now of much commercial significance unless to boat-hiring firms. But to the voyager, whether in cruiser, dinghy, rowing boat, punt or canoe, they still provide a pleasure and a challenge unequalled elsewhere.

101

5

RIVER-CROSSINGS

Fairford, Queensferry, Cambridge—three very different places but each owing its existence and its name to a river-crossing. Fairford stands on the Coln, a tributary of the Thames; the present bridge, with the mill at one end, is eighteenth-century. It replaced a bridge with four stone arches—and that replaced a fair ford. On the other side of the river from the mill is St Mary's Church, founded by a local cloth merchant, John Tame, who—so the story says—commanded a ship which captured a Spanish vessel bound for Rome. In the cargo was a large quantity of painted glass on its way to the Pope. Tame brought the glass back to Fairford and built the church to house it; the twenty-eight windows show the story from the Creation through the Old and New Testaments to the Last Judgement.

The 'Queen' of Queensferry, the ancient crossing of the Forth superseded by the 1964 Forth Road Bridge, was Margaret, wife of Malcolm Canmore. They used the ferry frequently when travelling from Edinburgh Castle to Dunfermline, and her corpse was ferried across on her last journey to Dunfermline in 1093. There had been a crossing here for about a thousand years. The monks of Dunfermline Abbey ran the ferry at one time; later it was decreed a sin to work the ferry on the Sabbath Day and a fine of 12 Scots shillings was exacted from the sinners. The fare charged was according to rank, from 3s 4d (17p) for a duke or viscount down to one penny for an ordinary person. This is the ferry of Scott and Stevenson, with the Hawes Inn at South Queensferry. Most of the ferrymen lived in North Queensferry, a community forming an integral part of Scottish history, symbolised by the names of the last vessels to work the crossing—*Mary, Queen of Scots*, *Robert the Bruce*, and *Queen Margaret* herself, the very last to sail.

And lastly Cambridge—capital of the only shire in England with 'bridge' in its name. It developed around the point where the Roman road from Colchester to Godmanchester—the Via Devana—crossed the River Cam. To protect the crossing a fort was built; around this a settlement grew up and a wall was built, and it became an inland port. Later, William the Conqueror built a castle to defend the town and in particular its bridge. Medieval Cambridge became wealthy, with quays and warehouses lining the river. It was the early college foundations that pushed the commercial centre away from the Cam and began to develop the riverside in an entirely different way. The old Roman crossing became the Great Bridge and later Magdalene Bridge, as it is today.

A ford, a ferry, a bridge—it almost seems to be a natural process. Look at the crossings of a single busy river and see how the pattern fits together. A recent survey has shown that there is evidence of well over 80 crossings of the Trent from Burton to the Humber, including 33 ferries, 18 fords, 17 road bridges, 11 railway bridges and 6 footbridges. There was a busy ferry at Walkerith, used by local traffic and by drovers travelling from Scotland to fatten their cattle in East Anglia before selling them in the London market. It was into this ferry that 'Mr Hall's servant', finding the Gainsborough ferry full, 'was so rash and imprudent as to leap his horse . . . and with the violence of the fall drove the poor people and their horses to the further side, which instantly carried the boat into the middle of the stream and overset it'. There were thirty people on board, and six were drowned. This occurred in 1761. A few years later a pamphlet described the Trent below Newark as 'an almost insurmountable barrier' because of 'delays to which all ferries are subject over navigable rivers', as well as the obvious dangers and difficulties. In 1791 Gainsborough's three-arched stone bridge was opened at a cost of £10,750. Walkerith Ferry lost most of its customers and the owner of Gainsborough's ferry received £300 compensation. Tolls were payable at this bridge until 1932 and the bridge remains today much as it looked when first built. The original Gainsborough tolls contain one oddity: a foot traveller was charged ½d (the same as a sheep), a cow cost 1d and vehicles between 8d (3½p) and 2s 6d (12p) according to size. But a hearse with a body was charged 13s 4d (67p), an empty hearse crossing at half that extortionate figure.

At Littleborough there was a ford, probably the lowest on the river, on the Roman road from Lincoln to Doncaster (now called Till Bridge Lane). It may have been made on the orders of Hadrian, about AD 120, slopes being cut down the banks and the crossing itself paved with stone retained by oaken stakes. It was removed in 1820 as it obstructed the navigation. This ford was on one of the main north-south routes, but it is likely that Harold and his forces used it on their way to defeat near

Ford on the Upper Thames. Fords on the Thames were almost obsolete when this picture was published, 1875

Hastings and later William crossed it at the same place heading northwards. In the sixteenth century a ferry supplemented the ford, operating until about 1900. No bridge was ever built at Littleborough but a rowing boat took passengers across until World War II. It was Dunham nearby that obtained the bridge, but not until 1832 when the Trent was spanned by 900 tons of cast iron. About 3 miles upriver at High Marnham, near the present power station, King John granted the monks of Rufford the right to use the ferry toll-free, a privilege also enjoyed by local residents in the early nineteenth century, when at Christmastide the ferryman and his dog were given a free meal of roast beef and plum pudding at the vicarage while the parson's dog was turned out of doors.

Cromwell lock and weir mark the head of the tidal Trent. Just below the lock is the site of a Roman bridge which existed probably between the second and sixth centuries. The remains of the bases of the piers of the bridge were finally destroyed when the river was deepened in 1884, but sightings showed that there were about seven piers of timber, lozenge-shaped, the framework being filled with stone laid on edge. The piers were over 30ft long and 10ft wide, and the base of the bridge was timber-framed. As with all the Roman bridges in England, the roadway was of wood, the width being estimated at 20-22ft.

There is no evidence of ford or ferry at Cromwell, but there were two fords a mile or so further up between North Muskham and Holme, each of them wide enough for thirty horses to cross abreast. In his survey of the river Jessop said that carriages crossed in up to 4ft of water. Following improvements to the river a ferry crossing was instituted, lasting until World War II.

A branch of the river takes the navigation through Newark, while the main river sweeps round the north west of the town. Hereabouts there are three old and important bridge sites. The first reference to a bridge at Newark, where there had already been a ford for several centuries, was in 1135. This was swept away by floods in 1486 and replaced by a bridge of oak and stone, with a timber parapet. This one was reconstructed in 1597 and extensively repaired in 1635, the ford being used at times. In 1768 Smeaton began to build a causeway between Newark and Muskham Bridges as the road was often flooded and boats had sometimes to be used. A few years later Newark Bridge was rebuilt in brick faced with stone, not very conveniently as, when the river was high, larger vessels had insufficient headroom to pass the arches. Apart from widening of the carriageway, the bridge has been little altered since.

Both Newark and Muskham Bridges were on the old Great North Road, which was becoming an important route by the mid-fifteenth century. By this time the bridge at Muskham was about 150 years old. These Trent crossings were hotly contested during the Civil War, when the Newark garrison, loyal to the king, held both bridges. The Parliamentary commander, Sir John Meldrum, crossed the main river by a bridge of boats, with 1,000 cavalry and 2,000 foot soldiers. The Royalists withdrew into Newark and Muskham Bridge was taken. Then a force under Prince Rupert advanced to relieve Newark and defeated part of Meldrum's army near the bridge of boats. Meldrum himself intended to escape over Muskham Bridge, but his own cavalry, having fled over it, destroyed it, leaving him to surrender. When Scottish troops arrived in 1645 they built a large earthwork, called 'Edinburgh' near the Muskham crossing, traces of which still survive. The bridge itself was rebuilt in 1652 but had a poor reputation for safety, traffic sometimes using a nearby ford in preference. That too had its dangers, the Newcastle waggon being swept away there in 1759. After the new causeway was made the bridge was repaired; during this operation the old York stage coach overturned, two of the six horses, the coach and the passengers all falling into the river, though no one was drowned. Crowds gathered by the bridge in 1828, expecting to see it carried away

Trent Bridge, Nottingham, above *c*1875, below *c*1850

by floods, but were disappointed; indeed, it lasted for a further ninety years, although latterly heavier vehicles were diverted to Kelham. It was replaced by the present bridge in 1922.

The third of the Newark area bridges, Kelham, was first referred to in 1225. This was also destroyed in the Civil War and not rebuilt until 1677. Eighty-five years later it was again rebuilt, not very well apparently, according to the number of complaints recorded. It was surveyed by William White in 1849, who said that there was so much rotting and decay that repairs would be a waste of money. A timber bridge was built to replace it; five years later this was demolished by a large sheet of ice, and the wreckage was sold for £231. Work on the present brick bridge began in 1855, and, despite criticism of its workmanship, it still carries traffic today.

Of the Trent between Newark and Nottingham it was said in 1869, 'it is believed that no similar instance can be found in the Kingdom of a rapid, broad, dangerous and frequently impassable river intersecting a county and stopping all intercourse (except by dangerous and inconvenient ferries) for 26 miles'. An iron and timber crossing at Gunthorpe was opened in 1875. This proved inadequate for motor traffic and was bought by Nottingham County Council who replaced it with a reinforced concrete bridge nearby.

The present Trent Bridge at Nottingham dates from 1871, although it has been widened since. The first bridge on the site was recorded in 924, and known as Hethbeth Bridge. Over the centuries it seems to have been rebuilt and repaired in a piecemeal fashion; Henry II had the southern part reconstructed with round-headed arches about 1156 and some gothic-style navigation arches were built between 1252 and 1275, at which period there was a chapel dedicated to St Mary on the bridge. A hundred years later a ferry was operating, profits from which were devoted to repairing the bridge. Soon afterwards Bridge Masters were appointed to raise funds for maintenance but the ultimate responsibility for its upkeep was spread over about six authorities in the county, each liable for a number of the arches, the bridge itself being outside the city boundaries. It was first referred to as Trent Bridge in 1564. In succeeding years various arches collapsed or were destroyed; in 1673 ominous reference was made to 'ould decayed trees' being cut down for repairing piles of the bridge. By the mid-eighteenth century the bridge consisted of five arches at the northern end, dating from 1684, three very old pointed arches, a segmental span replacing an arch that collapsed in 1636, two more pointed arches, a span rebuilt in 1725 and three more arches rebuilt in 1702. The total length was 668ft, with the river passing under the ten northern arches, and the width of the roadway was a mere 12ft. Subsequently some widening took place, but essentially this was the bridge that was demolished in 1871 when its replacement was opened.

In 1870 Wilford Toll Bridge, above Trent Bridge, replaced a ferry with a particularly high casualty rate, until it was closed to traffic in 1974. Much of the heavy traffic now uses the modern Clifton Bridge. Above Clifton there was a large number of fords and ferries, the ferries being especially perilous to drunkards. Once a Sawley ferryman, with three passengers, tried to sail his boat across the river and all were drowned. River improvements disposed of the fords, and the later ferries nearly all ceased by 1945. Harrington Bridge was opened at Sawley in 1792, the three river arches being replaced by steel spans in 1906, and a reinforced concrete bridge takes the motorway over the Trent. Wilden Ferry, first mentioned in 1310, for many years was recognised as the head of the Trent navigation; a bridge with five stone arches, described as 'elegant', was erected here in 1760, known as Cavendish Bridge after the Duke of Devonshire who held a mortgage on it. The central arch collapsed in 1947 and the bridge was later replaced by a new one made further downstream.

Legend says that Swarkestone Bridge was built by two sisters whose lovers were drowned when trying to ford the river. It replaced a structure known as the Bridge of Cordy (it may have been a wooden bridge held together by cords) which existed in 1204. For some centuries Swarkestone was the only bridge between Nottingham and Burton. Its total length was about a mile but the accounts of the total number of arches vary from twenty-seven to forty. It included a causeway, much of which remains, but the bridge over the river was demolished in 1797 when the present bridge was built. Willington Bridge is much newer, being opened in 1839 with five arches and a cattle arch at each end. Like many of the others it was a toll bridge; the toll board is in Repton church, where it was put in 1898 when Derbyshire CC took over the bridge and abolished the tolls. Church bells rang, there was a procession, and a celebratory dinner was eaten on the cricket fields of Repton, whose former headmaster had laid the bridge's foundation stone.

The bridge at Burton-upon-Trent may have been first built for the conveyance of stone across the river for the building of Burton Abbey. It was certainly existing in 1175. Like other medieval bridges it was maintained by gifts. It was repaired several times, having thirty-four or thirty-six arches, and was crossed by Mary, Queen of Scots on her last sad journey to Fotheringhay. The old bridge was demolished in 1864.

This journey up one of England's great rivers may give some slight idea of the history and variety of river-crossings. Because of the Trent's size, industrial importance and geographical location—and because of bank-improvement works—there are only a few traces of the many old fords and ferries and none of the really old bridges have survived. All over the country fords disappeared under schemes to improve navigation or drainage or as traffic increased they were replaced by bridges. Many of them were dangerous, particularly at night when their position might be mistaken, or in time of flood—as we were shockingly reminded in the spring of 1977 when a car was swept away at a ford when the River Kym was in spate and two people were drowned. While the suffix in a place-name indicates the presence of a ford at some time there were, of course, far more fords than survive in place-names; on the stretch of the Trent just described, only Shelford and Wilford preserve this element of their history in their names.

Ferry sites are easier to identify, often simply by the presence of a Ferry Boat inn. A good example is at the crossing of the Deben between Felixstowe and Bawdsey, where the ferry, still operating, gives its name to the locality and where the records go back to 1181. Owing to the tides the crossing was not easy. Until a steam ferry, which ran on chains laid

The ferry between Dartmouth and Kingswear on the Dart, 1957

on the riverbed, was launched towards the end of the nineteenth century, horses swam the river—the mixture of humans and horses on small ferryboats was fraught with potential dangers. But like others, the steam ferry proved uneconomic and was replaced by rowing boats and then by a motor boat.

The deeply indented coastline of Devonshire meant that communications were very dependent on ferries. Until 1774 Exeter was the lowest bridging point on the Exe and Sherborne Abbey, which owned land locally, ran a ferry service from Exmouth to Starcross from the twelfth to the sixteenth centuries. When the abbey was dissolved the ferry continued, being rented to the Drake family for 26s 8d (£1.33½) a year; in 1846 it was bought by the South Devon railway for £1,000. There was a medieval ferry at Teignmouth and another between Dartmouth and Kingswear across the Dart—the passenger fare for this one was only one halfpenny. There were at least three ferries across the

Tamar; Defoe used the crossing from Plymouth to Saltash, 'a little poor shattered town'. Like others, he did not enjoy the voyage: 'The Tamar here is very wide, and the ferry boats bad, so that I thought myself well escaped, when I got safe on shore in Cornwall.' The latest of the Tamar ferries, between Devonport and Torpoint, began not long before the age of steam, and a steam floating bridge was running from 1836. This crossing still operates.

The principal ferry in North Devon took passengers across the Taw-Torridge estuary from Appledore to the south end of Braunton Burrows. Richard Ayton, who accompanied the painter, William Daniell, on their *Voyage around Great Britain* and who wrote much of the text for this beautiful, illustrated book, described their crossings in the early nineteenth century while on their way to Ilfracombe.

> The wind and tide were foul, but the ferryman, utterly unmindful of these particulars, set his sail up and himself down, and quietly awaited the result. We did alter our situation, and gradually increased our distance from Appledore, but without approaching nearer to the place to which we were bound. The river is not quite a mile broad, so that when this singular method of getting over it had been prolonged for an hour, we considered ourselves justified in enquiring when we might expect to reach our port. Our phlegmatic boatman then first made us acquainted with a kind of misgiving that had long been gaining ground on his feelings, and had now terminated in a conviction that our sail had been perfectly useless and that nothing but hard labour could enable us to get over the water. He then applied himself to row and in an hour and a half more we landed on the opposite shore—3 miles from Braunton—no beds and all night sitting up in the pub.

In the past their users have had little that was complimentary to say about ferries. Defoe reckoned himself lucky to have arrived safely in Cornwall, but he could not bring himself to face the challenge of the Severn. Having arrived at the passage 'from a little dirty village called Aust ... the sea was so broad, the fame of the Bore of the tide so formidable, the wind also made the water so rough, and which was worse, the boats to carry over both man and horse appeared so mean, that in short time none of us cared to venture.' Some decades later, William Gilpin showed more courage at the same crossing. As his party arrived at the ferry-house they heard the boatman sounding his horn for the horses to be brought down to the beach, about a quarter of a mile below. Then the horn sounded again for the foot-passengers, 'and a miserable walk we had to the boat through sludge, and over shelving and slippery rocks. When we got to it we found eleven horses on board, and above thirty people; and our chaise (which we had intended to convert into a cabin during the voyage) flung into the shrouds. The boat, after some struggling with the shelves, at length gained the channel. The wind was unfavourable, which obliged us to make several tacks, as the seaman phrase them. These tacks occasioned a fluttering in the sail; and this produced a fermentation among the horses, till their fears reduced them again to order.' The voyage took nearly two hours, followed by another uncomfortable walk through the sludge. Gilpin had little confidence in the ferrymen, 'for what is done repeatedly is often done carelessly'; nor was he the only one, for, 'A British Admiral, who had lived much at sea, riding up to one of these ferries .. and observing the boat as she was working across the channel from the other side, declared he durst not trust himself to the seamanship of such fellows as managed her; and turning his horse, went round by Gloucester.' He described several disasters, in one of which a boat carrying sixty oxen sank and another when a gentleman's hat blew overboard and he seized the helm to turn the boat about to rescue it. In the ensuing struggle with the ferryman the helm 'got a wrong twist' and the boat instantly filled and sank. The hat's lining, it later transpired, was stuffed full of money. The Beachley-Aust crossing, the Old Passage as it was known (there being an alternative, but less used, New Passage a little further down the estuary), was surveyed by Thomas Telford and Robert Stephenson and taken over by a consortium who built piers and approach roads and introduced a steam packet as an alternative to the sailing boats. Disasters sometimes still occurred, as when a sailing ferry struck a row of piles and sank with several passengers and animals on board in 1855. Traffic diminished after the opening of the Severn Tunnel in 1887 and ceased altogether when the Severn road bridge opened in 1966, although in the last thirty-five years of operation the two diesel craft on the run maintained an accident-free record.

The Severn was one of the river barriers but its ferries never inspired the devotion of their users to the same extent that the Mersey ferries have done, particularly now that they are under threat. There have been at least eight main ferry passages across the Mersey, the Liverpool Ferry recorded in 1323 and the Priory of Birkenhead and its successors being granted by Edward III a charter 'for ever' to ferry men, horses and goods between the priory and Liverpool. Now there are only three ferryboats at work and they are said to be losing nearly £1 million a year. The number of passengers carried has dropped from 18½ million about twenty years ago to 3½ million in 1976. To save the ferries a Friends of the Ferries

111

A ferry on the Upper Thames, 1875. Under an Act of William and Mary, Thames ferries had to be at least 22½ ft long and 4½ ft broad. Tolls for horses were from 1 to 3 pence each, according to the different ferries.

Society has been formed with the support of MPs and councillors of all parties, arguing that the ferries have 'a cultural, historical and social as well as practical value'. The threat to the Mersey ferries has produced a widespread reaction. 'We love them,' said the MP for Liverpool Walton. Likewise the last of the many and ancient ferry services across the Humber, worked by the paddle-steamer *Lincoln Castle*, is in danger of extinction.

On the Upper Thames ferries in 1875 the standard charge for foot passengers was one halfpenny, as it had been for over 300 years. Horses were charged from 1-3 pence, and the usual ferry boat was a wide, flat-bottomed craft, rather like an over-sized punt with ramps at each end. Some were punted across; others, where there was little traffic on the river, were operated by hauling on a rope stretched from bank to bank. Sometimes there were landing stages for use when the river was running high.

Norfolk and the Fens were especially dependent on ferry crossings; Surlingham, Stokesby, Bramerton, Martham, Reedham, Oxborough, Southery and Ely are just a few of the places where ferries operated. Many of them were winched across along chains laid on the riverbed and worked by turning a handle on the boat. The larger ones could carry two or three horses and carts or motor cars. Mostly they were worked by the landlord of the inn on one or other side of the river. Reedham ferry still crosses the Yare but nearly all the others have ceased. The shortest ferry crossing was a matter of a few yards; the longest on a river must have been the Long Ferry, 20 miles from London to Gravesend, the fare for which was originally the traditional halfpenny, rising to 2d in the reign of Henry IV and to a shilling (5p) by 1790. Tilt-boats were used on the Long Ferry route in the seventeenth and eighteenth centuries; in 1737 they were limited to forty passengers. Soon after this date, decked boats were introduced but they retained the old name. The last of them, the *Duke of York*, was withdrawn in 1834, as it could no longer pay its way.

We have seen that the sites of many ferries and fords are indicated today by the bridges which replaced them. Because the superstructures of the Roman bridges in this country were built of timber, none of them has survived. It has been thought that the clapper bridges of Dartmoor and Exmoor were pre-Roman, but there is no evidence to support this. The thirteenth century seems to be the most likely period for the original construction of these bridges, which themselves succeeded fords or stepping stones. Tarr Steps, over the Barle on Exmoor, is the finest example of the clapper bridge, with its seventeen spans each consisting of a stone slab about 7ft by 4ft. The bridge is about 180ft long and is part of the Winsford Hill ridgeway. There is no telling how many times

Tarr Steps across the Barle in Somerset

The Monnow Bridge, Monmouth, engraved by W. Deeble from a drawing by H. Gastineau. This is now the only bridge of its kind in Britain

it has been repaired or rebuilt, but the 1952 floods, which destroyed so much of Lynmouth, carried away everything except one span, although the original stones were all replaced. The stone slabs that compose Postbridge over the East Dart are larger—15ft by 7ft—but the bridge itself is less than 50ft long. There is another clapper bridge over the Wallaford at Bellaford, about 40ft long, and the first bridge over the Teign is of the same type, although this one was made in the eighteenth century.

So it is not to the clapper bridges that we should look for our earliest examples of bridge buildings, not even to the one that seems to have strayed from the south west to cross the Leach at Eastleach Martin in the Cotswolds. Because of the rebuilding and widening that has taken place, it is difficult to know where to look. Elvet Bridge over the Wear in Durham was being paid for in 1225 and 1228, but Edwyn Jervoise reckons that the oldest part of the surviving bridge dates from the mid-fourteenth century. The Monnow Bridge at Monmouth was built at the end of the thirteenth century; its fortified gatehouse is the only one now remaining, but unfortunately its records have long been destroyed. Lincoln High Bridge is said to date in part from 1160; the present buildings upon it were erected in 1540 when the bridge itself was widened. There is a reference to shops on the bridge in 1391, when they were left by John de Sutton to his servant, John, in his will. Huntingdon Bridge over the Great Ouse is referred to in 1259 but seems to have been entirely rebuilt about 1370. It has lost the chapel that once stood on it. St Ives Bridge, 5 miles downriver, retains its chapel of St Leger, consecrated in 1426 when the bridge, originally of timber, must have been rebuilt. At Bury St Edmunds there is a very old crossing of the Lark; three pointed arches take the wall of the abbey precincts over the river, with a footbridge on the inside of the wall. It is possible that there was a timber footbridge on the outside, fitting into the buttresses. Firm dating of this structure is not possible; 1230 is the earliest suggestion, but it may be up to a hundred years later. And on the other side of the country there are superb medieval bridges over the Dee. In Chester there was a bridge over the Dee referred to in Domesday Book; the order for the present Dee Bridge was made in 1346, to replace a timber structure by one of stone. This bridge, which shows a good variety of shape in its seven arches, is particularly well documented; in its time it has carried a tower, houses and an arch and has been described as 'dangerous and unsightly' as well as beautiful. The other great medieval bridge is at Llangollen, a four-arch bridge dating from the mid-fourteenth century.

The ancient bridge over the Lark at Bury St Edmunds. The footbridge can be seen the other side of the central arch, in the abbey precincts

Before the Reformation, indulgences were sometimes granted by the Church to those who contributed to bridge-building and repairing. The standard rate, as it were, was an indulgence of forty days, and the issue of an indulgence may help to date the construction of a particular bridge. As an example, Edmund, Bishop of Exeter, granted an indulgence in 1413 for the building of Treverbyn Bridge, at St Neot near Fowey. The Reformation not only put an end to this practice but, possibly as a consequence of this, marked the end of the building of major bridges until the beginning of the Turnpike era about 1750, in certain parts of the country at least. Certainly in Cornwall no new important bridge was built between 1540 and 1750. In that county the oldest surviving bridge is probably Yeolm Bridge, over the Ottery, with two pointed arches dating from about 1350. Other fine early Cornish bridges include Greyston Bridge across the Tamar on the Launceston-Tavistock road, and Horse (or Hautes) Bridge, 14 miles down the same river. Both of these date from 1435-40. Wadebridge over the Camel replaced a ford about 1468; it is 320ft long with at present fifteen arches, similar in style to Bideford Bridge, and originally had a chapel at each end. Cornwall also has some clapper bridges over the Delank river;

their date cannot be ascertained, although it is unlikely that they are particularly ancient. One of the last and greatest of the early Cornish bridges is again over the Tamar, the six-arch bridge at Gunnislake, built of white granite between 1520 and 1530. Two especially notable bridges were constructed over the Tamar estuary in more recent times; Brunel's Royal Albert railway viaduct of 1859 and the concrete, wire and steel Tamar Bridge of 1961, with a central span of 1,100ft.

The oldest surviving Devon bridge crosses the Clyst at Clyst St Mary; it was rebuilt in 1310. Holne Bridge takes the Ashburton-Princeton road over the Dart; it has four arches of rough granite, and dates from the fifteenth century. Bideford Bridge over the Torridge was built a few years later with twenty-four Gothic arches of differing sizes and totalling 677ft in length. This bridge had a chapel in its earlier years and the tolls that used to be charged were devoted to education and other charitable purposes. It was built by Sir Theobald Grenville, the site, so legend says, being selected by an angel who appeared in a vision to the parish priest. Charles Kingsley described it as 'the very omphalos, cynosure, and soul around which the town as a body has organised itself', which could be said about many other bridges by other people, using perhaps less extravagant terms.

Four especially fine bridges cross the Dorset Stour. Three of them are medieval, at least in part. White Mill Bridge, described by Jervoise as 'by far the most beautiful in Dorset', has eight arches with a total span of 210ft. It was largely repaired in 1713. Sturminster Newton Bridge originates from about the same time. Crawford Bridge was medieval in origin but rebuilt in the sixteenth century. It has nine arches over the river and three brick flood arches. Iford Bridge, which crosses the Stour west of Christchurch, consists of several series of arches joined by causeways and provides a kind of compendium of bridge arch design from the seventeenth to the nineteenth centuries.

Neither Sussex nor Hampshire is particularly rich in old bridges. Stopham Bridge over the Arun—it carries A283—probably dates from the sixteenth century and is made of local sandstone. The taller central arch is likely to have been added for navigation. Redbridge, over the Test on the outskirts of Southampton, was a very important crossing in the Middle Ages, the first reference dating from 1226. The old bridge,

(*overleaf*) Bideford Bridge in the early nineteenth century. From a lithograph by L. Haghe, the original 'drawn from nature' by E. Turle. The bridge, about 740ft long, was built *c*1460 and has been widened several times. No two of its twenty-four arches are the same width

Radcot Bridge, from the Halls' *Book of the Thames*. It now crosses a backwater of the river, a newer bridge taking the roadway over the main channel

now bypassed, was built in the seventeenth century. Wiltshire, however, has a good variety, including a medieval four-arch bridge at Lacock, a medieval packhorse bridge over the Avon at Combe Bissett—like many other packhorse bridges this one has no parapets, thus giving extra room for wide loads—and the fourteenth-century bridge at Bradford-on-Avon, with its chantry that became for a time a lock-up, John Wesley being incarcerated therein for a night in 1757. In the next county, Wool Bridge in Frome dates from 1343. Somerset also has good examples of packhorse bridges; there is a well known one at Dunster over the River Avill and another across a stream at Allerford, between Selworthy and Porlock. And at Winsford in Exmoor there is a splendid collection of small bridges crossing the Exe and the Winn brook, six of them in all.

'The finest bridge in the south of England' was the honour bestowed on East Farleigh Bridge on the Medway about 2 miles above Maidstone. Made of Kentish ragstone it dates from the fourteenth century and has four pointed arches with a small extra arch to ease the angle of the approach road. It is something of a hazard to navigators as the nearby lock is not in line with the navigation arch of the bridge and newcomers to the river may find it difficult to negotiate. Teston and Twyford are other notable old Medway bridges.

The bridges of the Thames have been more often described and illustrated than those of any other river; John Pudney's *Crossing London's River* is a good example of the more recent studies. On the tidal Thames there are twenty-seven crossings today; until the first Putney Bridge in 1729 there was only London Bridge to supplement the ferries. And in 1729 the bridge of London was still the early thirteenth-century structure of Peter de Colechurch, which survived until Rennie's replacement was opened in 1831. Rennie's bridge was itself replaced in 1967 and now crosses a lake in distant Arizona. Nearly all the present-day Thames bridges above Teddington lock date from the eighteenth or nineteenth centuries. The oldest survivor is Radcot, 'a venerable relic of antiquity'. The early thirteenth-century bridge is the three-arch structure of local stone over what is now a backwater; the channel nearest the Swan Inn was cut in 1787 and crossed by a span of that date. 'On old Radcot Bridge', said Mr and Mrs Hall in their *Book of*

Bridge over the Nene at Wansford. At one time this used to carry the Great North Road

the Thames, 1859, 'is the socket of a cross which once towered above the primitive structure, in accordance with the old custom which invested bridges with a sacred character, and beside, or upon which, it was once usual to construct wayside chapels, for the purpose of affording the weary traveller repose while performing his religious duties.' New Bridge, near where the Windrush meets the Thames, used to be considered the oldest on the river; the present bridge is certainly handsome but was built in the fifteenth century to replace a bridge that itself was probably a little later than Radcot.

The maintenance of the more important bridges throughout the country was made the responsibility of the justices by an Act passed in the reign of Henry VIII. This meant that when a bridge fell into disrepair, complaints could be laid before the justices who could levy rates for repairs and see that the work was carried out.

On the old Great North Road is Wansford, where the bridge over the Nene, bypassed since 1928, bears evidence of the local justices' responsibility in the letters PM—Peterborough Magistrates—and the date 1577, still discernible. There was a wooden bridge at Wansford in 1221, certainly in poor condition in 1334 when pontage—the right to take tolls—was granted for three years. The most costly item to take across was a cartload of cloth, for 3d. Two thousand onions cost a halfpenny, and it is worth noting the evidence of trade in fish: 100 salt mullets and dried fish at 2d, 12 lampreys for 1d, a cartload of sea-fish for ½d, and one salmon or 1,000 herrings for a farthing. The wooden bridge was badly damaged by floods in 1571, and the present bridge was built in the next few years to replace it. The southern part of this had to be reconstructed in 1795, owing to damage by ice, and the thirteen arches were reduced to ten. A fine old inn, the Haycock, stands at the southern end of the bridge. The Nene is spanned by several good bridges, but the most splendid is Irthlingborough, built probably during the fourteenth century, now 270ft long with nineteen arches.

The oldest bridge in Norfolk is Bishop Bridge over the Wensum. This succeeded a wooden crossing that connected the priories of Norwich and St Leonard; it was built under a patent of Edward I and was the only direct entrance to the eastern side of the city. It was transferred to the citizens themselves in 1393 for them to maintain thereafter. In Suffolk, Toppesfield Bridge over the Brett near Hadleigh is a good medieval example, but although there are plenty of ancient bridge sites in East Anglia there are very few pre-Reformation bridges that have survived. One of them is a fine packhorse bridge at Moulton across the Kennett, built of flint, stone and brick and with four arches. This bridge is 60ft

Essex Bridge at Great Haywood, Staffordshire, in 1896. The two gentlemen taking a rest are Mr W. H. Duignan and Mr Robert Holden (Sir Benjamin Stone collection, Birmingham)

long but only 5ft wide between the parapets, about average for a packhorse bridge. Another medieval packhorse bridge on the eastern side of England crosses the Rasen, a tributary of the Ancholme, at West Rasen. This is only 4ft wide.

The old bridges of Derbyshire had a bad reputation; many of them were particularly narrow and looked unsafe, even if they were not. Bakewell and Sheepwash Bridges over the Wye are among the more substantial survivors, although both have been considerably widened. On the Staffordshire border is the well known packhorse crossing of the Dove at Milldale, Viator Bridge; 'Why, a mouse can hardly go over it!'

123

said Izaak Walton. Even narrower—only 4ft—but very much longer, is the packhorse bridge over the upper Trent at Great Haywood in Staffordshire, Essex Bridge, with fourteen arches and a total length of just over 300ft. This replaced a wooden bridge in the early seventeenth century.

Apart from Lancashire, the northern counties are generally rich in attractive and interesting old bridges. In Yorkshire there are two chantry bridges, at Wakefield on the Calder and Rotherham on the Don. The first chantry at Wakefield was founded in 1398 to provide a place of worship for the sick in time of the plague, so that others could use the parish church without fear of infection. This was replaced by a chapel in memory of victims of the Battle of Wakefield. Sir Gilbert Scott went to work on this in 1847, but the whole west front was removed and is now mouldering away in the grounds of Kettlethorp Hall. Much of Rotherham Bridge was demolished when a new crossing of the Don was made and the river diverted, but the chapel, dating from the late fifteenth century, and three arches of the medieval structure still endure. Like that at Bradford-on-Avon, this chapel also served for a time as a prison. Yorkshire also has a clapper bridge across the Aire at Malham; the same river is spanned by a very fine medieval bridge at Kildwick, near Skipton, and there are several other good examples crossing the Esk, Rye, Ure, Nidd and Wharfe. It is a pity that few bridge-builders were as considerate as S. Rogers and T. Trevers, who carved their names and the date, 1650, on Kexby Bridge over the Derwent.

Outstanding bridges in Northumberland include Warkworth Bridge over the Coquet, built at the end of the fourteenth century, with a tower or defensive gateway at the south end, the fifteen-arch Old Bridge at Berwick, 1624, and one of the most spectacular of all, Twizel Bridge across the River Till. This has a single arch of 90ft, 'greate and strong', as John Leland described it in the 1530s. The English artillery under the Earl of Surrey crossed here on the way to Flodden Field; the bridge itself, widened in the nineteenth-century, is probably of fifteenth-century origin. The earliest suspension bridge is across the Tweed in this county, the Union Chain Bridge, built in 1820. The Tyne at Newcastle was bridged by the Romans; the present Swing Bridge, built between 1868 and 1876, is on the same site, which was also occupied by stone bridges, the first built in the thirteenth century and then replaced in the 1770s. The Swing Bridge supplemented Robert Stephenson's High Level road and rail crossing, the first bridge of importance on which a power-driven

(*opposite*) The bridges of Newcastle-upon-Tyne, 1962

125

William Edwards's bridge at Pontypridd, engraved by R. Roberts from a drawing by H. Gastineau. This view has long been obscured by an ugly but more practical structure

pile-driver was used. Elsewhere in the northern counties there are medieval bridges over the Eden at Warcop and across its tributary the Eamont on the road from Penrith to Shap. Lanercost Bridge on the Irthing and Crook of Lune are two other outstanding examples of the craftsmanship of the bridge builder; the Lune also claims the Devil's Bridge at Kirkby Lonsdale, one of the finest of all.

For about 200 years, as we have seen, between the reigns of Henry VIII and George III the art of bridge-building went into decline. One of the first to give it renewed inspiration was a mason, William Edwards, who worked in South Wales and bridged, among other rivers, the Taff and the Towy. Edwards's bridge over the Taff at Pontypridd, which 'rises from its steep banks like a rainbow, is exceedingly beautiful and picturesque from every point of view'. The existing bridge was his third attempt; the first was a three-arch structure which stood for two and a half years until the piers were destroyed by the accumulation of debris brought against them by floods. Edwards realised that a single span was needed, but this collapsed before it was finished because of the weight thrown on the abutments. He rebuilt the arch to the same dimensions but lightened the weight by piercing the haunches with three holes of graduated size. The span, 140ft, was the largest single span of its time; the arch was built as the segment of a circle, with diameter 175ft and height 35ft. Early paintings and engravings show the beauty of the bridge in its mountainous setting, unspoiled by the development of the town of Pontypridd. But the proportions of the arch did not make it easy to use; in the words of Benjamin Malkin, 'the sober market-traveller is not recompensed for the toil of ascending and descending an artificial mountain by the comparison of a rainbow'. Its inconvenience no doubt contributed to its survival as it was supplemented by 'an ungainly rival' in the 1850s, which took off the traffic. In 1773 Edwards built a bridge in similar style but with a lesser span and only one hole at each end across the Towy at Llandovery, Dolauhirion Bridge, which can still be seen to good advantage.

William Edwards—whose son, David, and grandsons were also bridge-builders—was a stonemason and a farmer, but not an engineer. Thomas Harrison was an architect, and his Grosvenor Bridge at Chester has been described as 'the greatest of all British masonry bridges'. It has a single span of 200ft and the arch rises 42ft. From its opening in 1832 it took the traffic off the old Dee Bridge in the city. Grosvenor Bridge has a classical dignity, compared to the romantic appeal of the bridge at Pontypridd. But by the time it was built bridge-building was rapidly becoming the province of the engineer. The famous iron bridge across the Severn, which has given its name to its locality, was opened on 1 January 1781. The original design was by an architect, Thomas Farnoll Pritchard, but it was adapted by the ironmaster Abraham Darby III, in whose foundry at Coalbrookdale it was cast. In shape it resembles a masonry bridge and the details of construction derived from carpentry. But it was made of iron, symbolising the growing industrial importance of the area and of the country as a whole. Rapidly it became a tourist attraction, a magnet for painters and visitors from abroad. 'The noble Arch presenting itself to the inspection of the curious traveller', wrote an anonymous curious traveller on a visit to Coalbrookdale in 1801, 'whose massy curved ribs fill him with astonishment beneath which the river Severn glides its gentle current, & many Vessels of various sizes are moored along its shaggy banks. A road here leads under the bridge, where the traveller should not omit going; the ribs, covered with iron plates & connected with strong pillars, will prove an object at once majestic and beautiful; lightness vying with grandeur, & simplicity with Elegance.' It has been recently discovered that another bridge, constructed about the same time at Preens Eddy nearby, although known as the Wood Bridge was actually built with cast-iron ribs; this was replaced a few decades later by the present Coalport Bridge.

The skills of masonry and engineering were united in the work of Thomas Telford. In 1778 at, the age of twenty-one, he worked on Langholm Bridge; a few years later he was appointed Surveyor of Public Works for Shropshire and he built over forty bridges in that county, including Montford Bridge over the Severn, on a site where the first bridge was recorded in 1285, and an iron bridge with brick abutments at Buildwas, 2 miles above Ironbridge itself. After working on the Ellesmere and Shrewsbury canals, including a major contribution to the great Pontcysyllte aqueduct, in 1801 Telford moved to the Highlands of Scotland where he was responsible for the construction of several hundred bridges and over 900 miles of roads. Notable surviving bridges include Glenshiel, a splendid cast-iron bridge at Craigellachie with a single span of 150ft, a five-arch bridge over the Dee at Ballater, Ferness Bridge over the Findhorn, Dean Bridge, Edinburgh, across the Water of Leith, and Cartland Crags Bridge across the Mouse Water west of Lanark, with two piers 129ft high. Telford's later work included the iron Waterloo Bridge, carrying the Holyhead road across the Conwy at

Ironbridge across the Severn, now used as a footbridge only. The centre span is 100ft long

Betws-y-Coed, the great bridge over the Menai Straits, opened in 1826, and the smaller decorative Conwy Bridge beside the castle opened later in the same year. And in addition to the Shropshire crossings of the Severn, Telford designed the fine stone bridge at Bewdley—this earlier in his career, in 1798—the single span cast-iron bridges at Holt Fleet, north of Worcester, and Mythe, near Tewkesbury (which he considered 'the handsomest bridge to be built under my direction'), both with masonry abutments, and Over Bridge at Gloucester, again of stone and recently bypassed by a new crossing. Telford's contribution to the art and craft of bridge-building is greater than that of any other individual and was based on an understanding of proportion, the strengths, flexibility and appropriateness of materials, and of the power of water.

The subject, unlike the reader, is inexhaustible. Apart from one mention, nothing has been said of the extraordinary and fascinating collection of bridges on the Bristol Avon—Maud Heath's Causeway, the old bridges of Lacock, the packhorse bridge at Monkton, Pulteney Bridge at Bath, the Clifton suspension bridge and the new M5 crossing at Avonmouth. The Wye also has a wide range of good examples, including the excellent brick bridge at Bredwardine, the fifteenth-century crossing at Hereford, Wilton Bridge, opened in 1599 at Ross, the seventeenth-century Wye Bridge at Monmouth, a Telford bridge a few miles below, Chepstow Bridge and the recent Wye extension of the great Severn bridge taking the M4 into Wales. And what about the fine bridges over the Lugg, Llanrwst Bridge over the Conwy, Devil's Bridge over the Afon Mynach? We are very fortunate in the richness of our heritage.

6

RIVERS AND NATURAL HISTORY

Rivers and streams have their particular role in natural history. Water flowing in one direction determines the types of organisms that can exist in it. Within the variety of rivers there are certain general similarities; hence it is possible to talk of riverside plants or the birds of rivers and ponds. And of the making of books about fish, there is no end.

Perhaps we should look first, then, at fish. And we can start with one of the most remarkable happenings of recent years. Not so many years ago—in 1957, in fact—a survey of the 30 miles of the London Thames showed that no fish at all could be found there, with the exception of eels. A few years later the rebuilding of the principal sewage works on the river began, with the result that dissolved oxygen soon reappeared in the river water. Since 1964 records have been kept of the varieties of fish discovered in the Thames between Fulham and Northfleet. By April 1975, no fewer than eighty-three different kinds of fish had been notified. This total included common edible marine fish, such as herring, cod, haddock and mackerel, the fearsome sting ray, the unpleasant-smelling smooth hound shark, sometimes sarcastically called Sweet William, oddities such as the pogge and the lumpsucker, and rarities like the triggerfish. The Thames was once a famous salmon river, and a salmon or two and a few trout have returned to its waters. So have the lampern and the lamprey, popular items in the diet of the Middle Ages.

Among the freshwater varieties are all those familiar to anglers; barbel, bream, carp, chub, dace, perch, pike, rudd and tench. Wild goldfish, loach and ruffe have also been found. Mostly the fish are intercepted by the screens across the power-station intakes; in 1976 a sea horse appeared at Dagenham. The extraordinary number of varieties that have been recorded, with so many of the specimens in fine condition, is the best proof there could be of the restoration to health of the river, and the best possible tribute to the work of those engineers and biologists who set themselves the task of bringing the Thames back to life.

More people are drawn to the banks of our rivers by angling than by any other activity, but there is not much room these days for the little boy with his stick, string and garden worm wriggling on a bent pin. For so many anglers the sport has become a wholly organised activity, competitive and exclusive. 'The match fisherman', wrote a recent medal-winner, 'needs to become a precision machine, intent only on proving himself a cunning adversary to both the fish and his fellow competitors.' There are prizes to be won, sometimes exceeding £100, and bookmakers take bets on teams or individuals. Over £150 can be spent on basic equipment, and between £5 and £10 on bait for a single competition. And whatever the competitors may be feeling as they line the banks of the great match-fishing rivers of the eastern half of England—Great Ouse, Nene, Welland and Witham—what they are doing does not look much like fun. What is caught is kept, weighed and put back—to be caught again next week and the week after that, as far as anyone knows.

The great and growing popularity of angling is, of course, beneficial as far as the condition of the water is concerned, as it is in the interests of both anglers and the licensing authorities to keep the water as pure as possible. Some of the side-effects, however, are not so beneficial: the destruction of plantlife on the banks, for example, or the dangers to animals and birds caused by discarded nylon line, hooks and lead weights. There is no doubt that what is referred to in today's language as 'the multi-purpose use of water space' leads to conflict between the various interests, but, when it comes to the counting of heads, those who put angling as the foremost of their interests outnumber all the others. This helps to explain why the Regional Water Authorities have Fishery Officers, but not Navigation Officers, in their hierarchies. Fish-farming is now widely undertaken; the Southern Water Authority, for example, one of the smaller regional authorities, has a trout hatchery in Sussex and a coarse-fish hatchery in Kent; in the former, up to 100,000 trout are being raised at any one time.

To improve the sport of angling there has been much human intervention. Foreign species, such as the rainbow trout, have been introduced and naturalised, while some native species have been culled. The rivers which hold the largest numbers of the different breeds of fish are generally those in the east, south and south west. Those holding more than ten species include the Thames, Hampshire Avon, Exe,

Parrett, Severn, Warwickshire Avon and the Dee, while nine or ten species can be found in many rivers—Welland, Lee, Medway, Kentish Stour, Sussex Ouse, Dorset Stour, Brue, Wye and Yorkshire Ouse among them. At times attempts have been made to divide rivers into biological regions, from cascade reach through troutbeck, minnow reach and lowland reaches to the estuary. A 'typical' river, carrying a variety of species, could support eels and trout throughout the whole of its length. Salmon could ascend to the troutbeck region; grayling, dace and chub in the minnow and lowland reaches; pike, roach, perch, bream, tench, carp and rudd would be found in the lowland reaches only, and flounders, bass and others such could be caught in the estuaries. But there is no such thing as a 'typical' river and such a method of division is only a useful simplification.

Another way of examining fish distribution is by looking at the pattern over the kingdom as a whole. The rivers of east and south-east England do not support salmon and few of them contain sea trout—the Sussex Ouse and the Kentish and Suffolk Stours are exceptions. Pike and perch are not found in Scotland, West Wales or Cornwall; bream and tench are concentrated in East Anglia, the Midlands, the lower valleys of the Severn and Warwickshire Avon, and in Anglesey—though not elsewhere in Wales. The fish that you cannot escape wherever you go is the eel, as most anglers know who catch them when fishing for something else. Because of their well known way of life eels can penetrate into virtually any river; only rivers so polluted that they cannot maintain life cannot maintain eels.

Salmon and trout—the game fish—breed in the winter, and game fishing is a spring and summer activity at its best. The price of salmon is now so high that one might be excused for thinking that those seen on fishmongers' slabs, or consumed in restaurants, were only those surplus to the requirements of Scottish lairds, brought south from the Highland rivers by Rolls-Royce. In 1973, however, as a sample year, over 93,000 salmon were taken in the rivers of England and Wales, of which fewer than a quarter were caught by rod and line. The rest were netted; statistically they belong to commerce, not to sport. In England salmon are found in the Coquet and the Esk in the north east, and in many of the rivers of Hampshire and the South West. Severn and Wye, Usk, many Welsh rivers and the fast-flowing rivers of north-west England are also notable for salmon fishing.

Because of the way in which Scottish fishing is organised—if that is the word; 'carved up' some people might say—full statistics are difficult, if not impossible, to come by. Fishing rights on the great Scottish salmon

Game-fishing on the River Leny in Perthshire

rivers—Tweed, Tay, Dee, Don, Spey, Deveron and the others—can be privately owned or rented, can belong to hotels or to associations; the rental of a beat can be well over a thousand pounds a week, and there may be good commercial reasons for divulging as little information as possible about the number of fish actually caught. And it is only the fish that escape netting, both at sea, especially off Greenland where the Atlantic salmon feed, and in the estuaries, which do not succumb to the disease known as UDN and which are not killed or forced away by pollution, that remain to be caught by the single fisherman. It has been estimated that the proportion of netted to rod-caught salmon in Scotland is higher than the figures quoted above for England, although the greatest number of netted fish, proportionately, is caught in the rivers of Northumberland.

Trout, of course, are more widespread than salmon; in the past few years there have been enormous developments in trout-farming, to supply especially the reservoirs and enclosed lakes. The Hampshire chalk streams, Avon, Test and Itchen, are among the most favoured rivers. Trout weighing up to 16lb have been recorded as being caught in the Itchen; the water of the Itchen is high in calcium and the river generally has a good flow. There is a similarly high calcium content in the water of the Dove, a limestone river. Conditions in the Yorkshire Dales and in the south west of England are also particularly suitable, but the trout is a very adaptable fish and can survive in the mountain streams of Scotland and the cold tributaries of the Upper Tees as well as in the warmer waters of southern England. The trout seems to have been Izaak Walton's favourite fish; he refers, as a notable curiosity, to the 'Fordidge' trout—the sea-trout of the Kentish Stour that runs through Fordwich—as being 'the rarest of fish', many of them near the bigness of a salmon, but only one of which he knew of had been caught by rod. And the dangers of over-fishing were pointed out as long ago as 1496, by Dame Juliana Berners in her *Treatyse of Fysshynge wyth an Angle*. She was also well aware of the delight of the sport, how close it brings man to nature. 'And if the angler take fysshe,' she says, 'surely thenne is there no man merier than he is in his spyryte.'

Birds, as well as anglers, take fish. The heron especially is a model of patience to any angler. Herons nest in trees near water, or in reed-beds; there are heronries in all areas of the British Isles. Eels, frogs and small mammals are included in the heron's diet and the birds return to the same heronry for several years. Equalling the heron in skill, though using an altogether different technique, is the kingfisher, which lives off small fish, such as minnows and gudgeon, and water-insects. Dependent entirely on obtaining its food supply from water, the kingfisher may starve in severe winter conditions when ice cuts it off from its larder. Kingfishers nest in holes which they bore in river banks; they wait on overhanging branches and dive on their prey. More like the fly-fisherman in its method is the dipper, which wades about in the hill streams of Scotland, northern England, Wales and the South West, sometimes walking upstream under water, sometimes (unlike the fly-fisherman) swimming. Tadpoles, minnows and insects are all part of the dipper's diet.

Other interesting waterside birds include the warblers, little brown birds often victimised by the cuckoo. Both reed and marsh warblers are mimics; the latter seems to have a keener ear but is rarer, being found mostly in the valleys of the lower Severn and the Warwickshire Avon. The reed warbler builds its nest by suspending it between stems of reeds a few inches above water level. All the warblers are summer visitors; the

Reed Warbler, chicks and nest

sedge variety is the most widespread and does not necessarily confine itself to sedge.

Reed-beds support a variety of birds of differing colours and sizes, of which many can be seen at the RSPB reserve at Minsmere in Suffolk. These include the bittern, master of the art of camouflage and famous for its boom. Bitterns were victims of the marsh and fen drainers; they disappeared from England altogether in the mid-nineteenth century but returned to the Broads some fifty or sixty years later. Under the auspices of the RSPB they are now also breeding in Lancashire, at

Leighton Moss, and in North Wales. Marsh harriers and avocets breed at Minsmere; so do bearded tits, which are Dundreary-moustached rather than bearded and reedlings rather than tits.

The various reserves maintained by the RSPB and the Wildfowl Trust, including, as well as those already mentioned, Slimbridge by the Severn, Havergate Island and Welney on the Ouse Washes between the New and Old Bedford rivers, have attracted enormous numbers of water birds. A count at Welney in February 1975 totalled 57,000, mostly wigeon, but with teal, mallard, pintail and pochard in thousands, hundreds of tufted ducks and shovelers, smaller numbers of goldeneye and smew and nearly a thousand Bewick's swans. Among the rarer birds at Welney are whooper swans, black-tailed godwits, ruffs and black terns, and there are also the far commoner species—yellow wagtails, lapwings and redshank, and short-eared owls. Observation conditions are luxurious—no lurking in the undergrowth, getting cold and wet feet, but sitting in an observation hide, centrally heated and fully equipped. At Welney and Slimbridge in winter you can watch the wildfowl by floodlight, a remarkable experience. The birds have returned to the Fens, still targets but now of the camera rather than the gun. There are few left now of the old breed of bird-lover who knew so well the habits and habitats of the wild duck and boasted of their bags of a hundred or more on a winter's morning. And the monstrous old punt guns are now prized antiques or museum pieces. A total of seventy-eight duck in three shots was claimed by one old expert; the same man claimed sixty-eight green plover with three shots and to have netted nearly 800 plover in six days. His most effective single shot with a punt gun destroyed forty-eight wigeon. One wonders, at times, when reading the exploits of the old wildfowlers, how any birds survived. Some, like the bustard, did not, and any bittern foolish enough to try to return to East Anglia in the second half of the nineteenth century seems to have been promptly shot. It is not easy to understand the sense of values of the wildfowlers, who so loved and admired the creatures they so prodigally slaughtered. For many of them, we should remember, it was their livelihood, but not for all. The others were sportsmen, or so they described themselves.

However selective in their shooting they claimed to be, the wildfowlers of the past can hardly be regarded as conservationists or protectors of wildlife, except insofar that it was in their interest to preserve the conditions in which wildfowl could survive. As predators they had their rivals. H.W. Wheelwright, who wrote under the pseudonym of the 'Old Bushman' in the 1840s, after recounting the

Approaching wildfowl with a stalking-horse. H. R. Robertson drew his representation in 1875 from the only example he found in regular use. The original stalking-horse, according to Gervase Markham writing in 1595, was

> . . . some old jade trained up for the purpose, who will gently, and as you will have him, walk up and down in the water which way you please, plodding and eating on the grass that grows therein. You must shelter yourself and gun behind his fore-shoulder, bending your body low down by his side, and keeping his body still full between you and the fowl. Being within shot, take your level from before the fore part of the horse, shooting, as it were, between the horse's neck and the water . . . Now, to supply the want of a stalking-horse, which will take up a great deal of time to instruct and make fit for this exercise, you may make use of any piece of old canvas, which you must shape into the form of a horse, with the head bending downwards, as if he grazed. You may stuff it with any light matter; and do not forget to make if of the colour of a horse, of which brown is the best . . . It must be made so portable that you may bear it with ease in one hand moving it so as it may seem to graze as you go.

Addition of horns to a stalking-horse turned it into a stalking-cow.

joys of shooting snipe, mallard and teal refers with some scorn to 'the prying eye of the collector'. 'One of the prettiest of all the little fen birds was the bearded tit', he wrote, 'which bred in the reed-beds near the mere; and so eagerly were the birds and nests sought after by our collectors, that every year it was becoming more rare, and by this time like many other of our rarer species is probably extinct.' He describes with affection 'the graceful and airy motion of a family of these birds flitting among the reeds after each other, in the manner of a long-tailed tit down a tall hedgerow, or balancing themselves on the reeds, their bell-like note ringing through the clear winter air'. Then in the last sentence of his paragraph we glimpse the odd sense of values. 'They remained in the fen during the whole year; and were it not that the gunner was forbidden to shoot among the reeds in the winter, on account of the damage the shot would do, they would probably have all been shot out long before my day.'

Yes, it is odd, and in this respect today's changed attitude towards wildfowl—and wildlife in general—is doubtless preferable. The changed attitudes are not only personal but official; we have our Nature Conservancy Council, and everyone interested in wildlife is alive to the dangers of pollution, whether caused by industrial waste, drainage of chemicals from agricultural land, sewage, or simply the dumping of unwanted but poisonous materials. The NCC reminds us that by improving waterways in one respect we may damage them in another; more efficient land drainage and improvements for the sake of navigation by dredging and tidying of banks may result in the destruction of rare plants and the habitats of birds and small animals.

The balance of nature can, of course, be tilted by creatures other than man, though not to the same extent. Two aliens, both escapees from fur farms, prey upon wildlife and are likely to have a marked impact on the areas where they operate. The North American mink is becoming established by rivers and lakes; water voles, fish, birds and insects compose its diet, but no creature appears to devour the mink in return. The other alien is the coypu from South America, a large rodent from which the fur known as nutria is obtained. Unlike the mink, the coypu is not carnivorous, but feeds extensively off waterside plants, and it burrows into river banks with the danger of undermining them. Strong efforts have been made to confine the coypu to East Anglia, but it is a formidable—and rather unattractive—little animal; not so little, in fact, as it can grow about 2½ft in length and can weigh well over a stone.

While both mink and coypu are under attack there has been a recent rally to the defence of the otter. For centuries the otter was regarded as the angler's chief enemy, and the sport of otter-hunting was as respectable as hunting the fox. More recently the otter suffered from poisonous agricultural chemicals and from the greatly increased use of rivers for recreational use. Public sympathy and understanding for the animal were aroused by writers such as Henry Williamson and Gavin Maxwell and this has been translated into action by the formation in 1971 of the Otter Trust, which is concerned with the conservation of otters throughout the world. Otters are now being bred under protection near Bungay in Suffolk, and efforts to have the animal legally protected are meeting with success at last. From January 1978 the otter became a protected animal. Philip Wayre, founder and director of the Otter Trust, sums up the prospects clearly. 'The future of the otter as a wild animal in England depends on the understanding of all who use

Otter, at last placed under a Conservation Order in November 1977

our waterways for whatever purpose. If it can be granted legal protection and a few undisturbed backwaters in which to live, the otter may survive. If not, it is doomed to disappear from our countryside forever.'

'Each man kills the thing he loves,' wrote Oscar Wilde, in a different context. We have seen how this can apply to the wildfowler and the collector. Botanically, one of the most interesting areas of the country is Upper Teesdale. 'But', says the Durham County Conservation Trust, 'one of the main threats to the rare plants is the naturalist himself; other offenders are parties of pupils or students led by someone who should know better, but unfortunately knows what to look for and where to find it. Many thousands of plants have ended their life, forgotten, in a tin box or a polythene bag; and indiscriminating collecting must stop. The plant hunter must follow the big game hunter, and exchange his plastic bag for a camera and be very careful where he puts his feet and tripod!' This speaks for itself. It was in Upper Teesdale, however, that conflicts of interest came to a head a few years ago. The River Tees rises on the south side of Cross Fell; for a few miles it marks the boundary between Cumberland and Westmorland, being joined by two tributaries, Trout Beck and Crookburn Beck. It heads southwards, running fast, across part of the Whin Sill, then, until a few years ago, the pace slowed, the river widened and deepened, forming a pool known as the Weel. Then there is a bridge, and below that the waterfall, Cauldron Snout, falling 200ft in seven great leaps. But it is not quite like that now. The Weel has gone; in its place is the Cow Green Reservoir, and above Cauldron Snout is a dam through the foot of which the Tees is piped before it descends the falls. Beneath the reservoir is part of Widdybank Fell, described by the NCC as an area of 'international botanical importance'.

Industrial Teesside needs the water which the reservoir collects, stores and supplies, and it is true that the lake is already beginning to look like a natural element of the landscape—if you stand with your back to the dam. Specimens of many of the rare arctic and alpine plants were collected before they were drowned and a full study of the area was made. About 15,000 plants were removed of the 130 varieties present in the acreage flooded; the botanists say that the greatest loss was 'of the vegetation mosaics composed of patches of rare and common plant communities'. Now three factors have combined to bring far more visitors to the area than ever before. One is the publicity arising from the controversy over the making of the reservoir, another is the new lake itself, and the third is the greater national interest in the countryside in general, together with increased mobility consequent upon increasing

140

affluence. In 1974, about 42,000 people visited Cauldron Snout and Cow Green. A discreet car park has been constructed and a made-up path now leads the visitor from there to the top of the waterfall. To some, this may seem a violation of the landscape, but without these amenities the more delicate plants and habitats would soon be destroyed by tyres and trampling feet. The rarer plants include moonwort, spring gentian and northern bedstraw; there are three types of sedge, yellow, carnation and the rare false sedge; among them grow birdseye primrose and butterwort. By the Tees itself grows the shrubby cinquefoil, able to survive even in times of flood, and a large number of plants that grow in limestone regions. It is thought that some of the plants of Upper Teesdale have been growing there since the melting of the glaciers at the end of the Ice Age. But it is less than a hundred years ago that the Weel was described as 'White and weird and still, where scarcely even the winds can reach it; and so deserted is it that not so much as a single wild fowl breaks the surface of its ghastly calm'.

Another example of an area where interests conflict, although on a smaller scale, is Wicken Lode in Cambridgeshire. The lode, a little more than a mile long, is a branch of Reach Lode; both of these channels are probably of Roman construction and drain into the Cam. Wicken Lode runs through Wicken Sedge Fen; owned by the National Trust, a natural sanctuary of great importance, particularly to botanists and entomologists, with about 300 species of flowering plants, 700 varieties of moth and butterfly, including the swallowtail, and some 5,000 kinds of insects. Paradoxically, owing to peat shrinkage in the surrounding area, water has now to be pumped up into the fen instead of drained off it. The conflict here is between boat-owners and conservationists, the former wishing to preserve rights of navigation while the latter want to exclude all powered craft on the grounds that propeller action and wash cause turbidity, which in turn causes damage to habitats, and that the boats may also contribute to chemical pollution. Here a compromise may be effected by allowing boats to use most of the lode but not all of it, giving the scientists time and opportunity to examine the differences between the navigable and non-navigable stretches. There is a similar clash of interests not many miles away, between those who wish to extend the navigation of the River Lark and those who want to keep boats out of a part of the river especially rich in natural history. The arguments against boating are sometimes strong, but there is no denying that on occasions the passage of boats can be positively helpful by clearing weed growth that would otherwise clog or choke the waterway, or by obliging the authorities to clear the stream on their behalf. Weed-cutting on the Lark

Marsh helleborine, an orchid found in calcareous fenland and sometimes in coastal sand dunes

enabled bur-reed and arrowhead to become established.

It is difficult, if not impossible, to make general remarks of any value about the natural history of rivers. Some rivers have been the subjects of scientific studies; R.W. Butcher surveyed the plants of the Itchen, for example, finding water crowfoot and the lesser water parsnip where the stream was fastest, the marestail and the bur-reed in slower reaches, and Canadian pondweed and starwort where the water ran most slowly. To allow the stream to flow and fishing to take place, the vegetation had to be cut back in the slowest reaches. These were the most common plants in the river, and one would expect to find these plants dominant in rivers of similar profile flowing across similar ground. An attempt to divide 'a river' into five zones, based on the findings of Butcher, was made some years ago, and has a certain usefulness with some correspondence to the previous mentioned division of a river into reaches where particular species of fish exist. The first zone is the headstreams and highland waters, where the flow is swift; mosses and liverworts are the major plants and there will be few, if any, plants of any height. The second zone is where the flow is fairly rapid; the river runs over a rocky bed but there are patches of gravel where the water crowfoot can grow, with a few plants of a similar type. In the third zone the flow is moderate; water crowfoot is still predominant but is joined by the bur-reed, Canadian pondweed and various kinds of *Potamogeton*. The flow of the river is moderately slow in the fourth zone and slower still in the fifth. In these zones there will be a wide variety of plantlife, with water crowfoot far less important. This zonal division can at best be only an approximation; as Macan and Worthington point out in *Life in Lakes and Rivers*, the Tees above Cauldron Snout—this is before the construction of the reservoir— provides 'a pretty example of the sort of exception to the general plan which is to be found in almost any river', as there is a slow stretch only a few miles from the source of this 100-mile river with vegetation characteristic rather of the third zone. Then the flow accelerates, and we are back, as it were, to zones one and two.

So, for those investigating the plantlife of a particular river, where you are determines what you will find. The tree most often associated with flowing water is the willow, and if a boatman or riverside walker runs into trouble he or she may be grateful for the help a willow, according to Culpeper, affords. The leaves, bark and seed can be used to stop bleeding from the nose or mouth; they can stop you from being sick or can prevent consumption. Rubbed with pepper and drunk in wine, the leaves also help the wind colic. And—should you be a member of a mixed party and concerned about your virtue—it is worth remembering that 'the leaves bruised and boiled in wine, stayeth the heat of lust in man or woman, and quite extinguisheth it, if it be long used'. If you are in zone one of a river, you would seek, naturally enough, for liverwort if your liver was diseased; it would also help 'to stay the spreading of tetters, ring worms and other fretting and running sores and scabs'. Further downstream, brooklime and watercress are good for the blood; they also 'provoke urine, and help to break the stone and pass it away'. If you have bruised your kidneys or suffer from St Anthony's Fire, search for Crab's Claw (pond weed and fresh-water soldier are among Culpeper's alternative names). Rushes of any kind, however, have no medicinal value, so you may as well leave them alone.

7

LOCKS, WEIRS AND DAMS

You can find what may well be the oldest surviving waterway structure in the country at Alresford, near Winchester. It is an embankment or dam, constructed by the order of Godfrey de Lucy, Bishop of Winchester, to create a reservoir designed to supply additional water to the River Itchen, thus enabling the river to be made navigable from Alresford to Southampton. The dam, 78yd long and 20ft high, was built about the year 1200 and the area of the original reservoir was about 200 acres, fed by the River Alre and another stream. Today this is Alresford Pond, extending over some 60 acres, and the bishop's embankment carries a road along its top. Having made the Itchen navigable, the bishop was granted by King John the right to levy tolls. Making the Itchen navigable must have needed the construction of staunches of some kind, but for how long the river remained usable is not known. It was reopened about 1710, with several straight cuts and locks, and remained in use until 1869.

Small weirs or dams were common sights on rivers and streams by the time Bishop Godfrey built his large embankment. Unless the current was constant they were necessary for the building up of a sufficient head of water to work a watermill, and there were several thousand of these in operation by the thirteenth century. There were also the fish-weirs, not generally permanent structures but of great importance in earlier times when freshwater fish was, as we have seen, an essential part of people's diet. On navigable, or potentially navigable, rivers, the mill-dams and fish-weirs were the places where interests clashed.

The compromise that was devised—no one can say precisely when—was a weir with a removable section—planks of wood that could be removed manually when a boat needed to pass, and then replaced. A development from this was the fitting of the planks into a frame that could be raised and lowered on the principle of the guillotine. Or a pair

A weir with movable bridge. H. R. Robertson describes the construction as follows:

First the sill or fixed beam, laid securely across the bottom of the stream; then, directly over this, but considerably above the surface of the water, is placed a second but movable beam. Against and in front of these parallel beams a set of loose boards is placed upright and close together like a door. These loose boards are called paddles, and the long handles with which they are furnished rest against the upper beam, the pressure of the stream serving to hold them in their places. Between the paddles are placed upright supports termed 'rimers': and when a second set of paddles is employed over the first to obtain a greater depth of water, this set is called the 'overfall' . . . In our illustration the man who is putting down the paddles is standing on the movable part, called the swing-bridge. It revolves on a pivot close to the edge of the water, and the weight is balanced by the increased thickness of the beam at the landward end, on which is often placed a great stone or other heavy substance. The upper beam and hand-rail across that part are, of course, removed before the bridge is swung round, and it is for this purpose that the two handles which may be noticed are added

of swinging gates could be inserted into the weir. These removable sections were called staunches, flashlocks or watergates, and they were the means by which navigation was made possible on rivers until the introduction of the pound lock in the mid-sixteenth century. And, despite all their disadvantages, some of them persisted in use until the present century. But today not one of them remains in working order and there are comparatively few traces of them to be found.

Flashlocks were used on the Thames, Wey, Lee and some minor tributaries, on the Kentish Stour, the Rother, Ouse, Arun and Itchen in the south, on the Parrett and Tone in Somerset, the Wye, Lugg, Stour and Warwickshire Avon in the west Midlands, on the Derbyshire Derwent and the Soar, and on the Nene, Great Ouse and several of its tributaries and the Suffolk Stour in East Anglia. On these rivers, the sites of more than eighty flashlocks have been traced. The flashlock was not simply a device to enable boats to negotiate weirs already in place; they were often installed for the sole purpose of the navigation. In *The Thames Highway*, F. S. Thacker quotes an early eighteenth-century writer. 'To remedy the want of water the use of Locks was happily invented, which are a kind of wooden machines placed quite a-cross the Current, and dam up the water. By this artifice the River is obliged to

A staunch near Brandon on the Little Ouse, 1890. The operator ascended the ladder to turn the large spoked wheel

(left) Barnwell Staunch on the River Nene, 1931;
(right) guillotine gate on a disused lock on the upper Lark at Icklingham

rise to a proper height till there is depth enough for the barge to pass over the shallows, which done, the confined Waters are set at liberty.' This writer commented that the voyage between Lechlade and London cost the bargemen nearly £14 in charges payable at the locks which were privately owned. In many instances, the owners were millers who wanted to control the flow of the river in their own interests. The problems are illustrated in the statement of a bargeowner in 1865, also quoted by Thacker:

If we have boats lying at Oxford to wait and go down the River, every Tuesday and Friday the millowners are obliged to draw for so many hours and let it run through the (flash) locks: we go five miles beyond Oxford and there the water is purchased. A man is sent forward to the next lock to wait there so many hours; the man goes on again, and so the water goes down with the boats. The water would accumulate to a certain height; when it got to that height I should draw that lock, and start off with the boat. I should send a man on to the next lock, and the miller who has the care of that lock is obliged to keep it closed for such a time. It has the effect of flooding the country frequently, from Lechlade to Oxford frequently. The man stands at the lock till the water comes down, and then, when the boats come down to that lock it is drawn, and the boats go down to the next pound.

Clearly it was a slow, tiresome and uneconomic business. It was also wasteful of water, and sometimes flashes left the river above almost dry. The flash helped the boat heading downstream on its way, but provided a difficult obstacle to the one travelling up. In this instance, enough water had to be let through for the lower level to rise sufficiently so that the boat could be hauled or winched through against the onrush of water.

On the busier navigations, flashlocks or staunches were eventually superseded by pound locks. On the lesser navigations—the Sussex rivers and some of the Great Ouse tributaries, for example—the navigation and the flashlocks were abandoned simultaneously. Their remains are little more than vestigial. The results of a survey of flashlocks were published in *Industrial Archaeology* in 1969 and 1970. The authors gave details of what relics there were and commented that 'though many flashlocks

The first lock on the Thames, near Lechlade, 1859. 'It is rude enough to be picturesque', wrote Mr and Mrs Hall

will no doubt moulder peacefully for years, more are at the mercy of floods, river authorities and even restoration societies, as the case of the lower Avon shows'. Today there is even less to be seen, and the best idea of what these constructions were like can be gained from old engravings and photographs. The present-day investigator need waste no time in looking for impressive monuments to the old days of navigation; the most he will see is a brick or stone-walled chamber with grooves and perhaps a bit of a gate-post or a hinge. The last of the guillotine-type staunches, at Bottisham Lode, was removed in 1970; the brick chamber can be found but the woodwork has rotted and the ironwork was taken away by the river authority for preservation.

We have seen that the first pound lock in Britain was built on the Exeter Canal by John Trew in 1563. The second was built at Waltham on the River Lee a few years later. There were two, possibly three, on the Thames by 1632, and the remains of the oldest survivor can be found at Abingdon, where the original navigation channel bypassed the town, taking the course of what was called the Swift Ditch. Here, on what is now a backwater, is the chamber of Swift Ditch lock—or Turnpike as it was known—constructed between 1624 and 1635. Later in that century pound locks were built on the Wey and the Great Ouse. During the following century pound locks became more common, although there was some opposition to them as being inconvenient and wasteful of water. The problem was that while several boats could make use of the same flash, only one or two could use a pound lock at a time. The canal builders had no doubts, however, and from the opening of the canal age the pound lock became the norm on the new navigations at any rate. But on some of the rivers—the Little Ouse, for example—old staunches were replaced by new ones, not by pound locks. Here the first staunch was built in 1742; this was followed by six more and between 1827 and 1835 they were all rebuilt. On the Little Ouse, as on many other rivers, the gates were normally kept closed, being opened only when a boat needed to pass through, although in times of flood they were kept open all the time. Sometimes, as at Tempsford on the Great Ouse, the gate was always kept open. Here the staunch was placed above a ford; the gate would be closed for a head of water to be built up to carry a boat over the ford, and then opened again after it had passed

Some of the earlier pound locks on rivers were turf-sided, as on the Wey and the Kennet, but mostly they were made similarly to those on canals of stone and brick. Most river locks have mitre gates at each end, although the Great Ouse, Cam, Nene and Yorkshire Derwent locks have a guillotine gate at one end. Only on the Nene are the guillotines

149

Remains of a lock gate on the Suffolk Stour. The once navigable cut is now overgrown; the last barge voyaged to Sudbury in 1916

at the tail of the lock. Three of the Nene locks are of radial type, where the guillotine gate goes over and above instead of straight up and down. And whereas the Great Ouse guillotines are electrically operated by the lock-keeper, on the Nene the boatman has to wind them down and up himself—in that order as they are normally left open because they are elements of the river's system of flood-control.

It is the Thames which boasts the largest and the smallest lock in current use, the barge lock and the skiff lock, both of them at Teddington. But there is no standard size for river locks in the same way that there is on the narrow canals, and the navigator should be careful to check the dimensions of the locks he intends to pass, and their method of operation, before starting a voyage. This particularly applies to the Middle Level Navigations where the locks were designed for fen lighters and 46ft is about the maximum length for any craft intending to cruise throughout the system.

The remains of locks can be found sometimes in what seems the most unlikely places on rivers where serious navigation at any time seems at first inexplicable. Rowing along the Western Rother in 1916, P. Bonthron found the sites of seven derelict locks, around which he had to carry his boat. The Sussex Ouse had eighteen locks, last used for commercial navigation in the 1860s. Wandering through rural

Leicestershire is the River Wreak, a tributary of the Soar. You can find it on the northern side of the A607 from the outskirts of Leicester to Melton Mowbray. Almost all the side roads heading north or north west off the A607 take you across the river, and by many of the bridges you can see the crumbling remains of locks. A word about the history of the Wreak explains their presence. In the late 1770s, the Erewash Canal and the Loughborough Navigation were both operating successfully; this led the people of Melton Mowbray to look at the prices they were paying, especially for coal, and to agitate for a water connection to their town. In 1791 an Act was obtained authorising the making of the Wreak, and part of the Eye, navigable, and the Melton Mowbray Navigation, as it was called, was open by 1798 at a cost of about £45,000, nearly 15 miles long with twelve locks able to take boats up to 14ft 6in beam. The navigation was extended further a few years later by the wholly manmade Oakham Canal. The canal was not a success, being expensive to construct and short-lived; it was abandoned in 1846. Until that year, in which the railway from Melton to Syston was also opened, the Melton Mowbray undertaking had done quite well, dividends rising to 10 per cent with 40,000 tons being carried in its best year. With the opening of the railway, however, trade began to leave the Wreak,

Crumbling remains of a lock on the River Wreak (Melton Mowbray Navigation), photographed in the dry summer of 1976

despite drastic reductions in tolls. By 1862 the company was trying to sell out, but nobody would buy. On 1 August 1877 the navigation was formally closed; the wharves and warehouses have gone and only the lock remains to remind us of the Wreak's commercial past.

We can make a comparison here with the Warwickshire Avon. This river was made navigable for barges between Tewkesbury and Stratford in 1639 by William Sandys of Fladbury. He built thirteen locks altogether, both flashlocks and pound locks; later in the century six more were added on the upper river. It did not prove satisfactory to administer the river as one single navigation; Evesham marked a convenient division between the lower and upper reaches and the Lower Avon was bought by George Perrott, also of Fladbury, who improved it in the 1760s. When the Stratford-upon-Avon Canal was opened, the upper Avon became closely associated with it. In the nineteenth century the Lower Avon was leased to the Worcester & Birmingham Canal Company for some years, while the Upper Avon passed through the hands of various railway companies until the GWR eventually refused to maintain it or even to take tolls. In 1875 the Upper Avon traffic ceased. The Lower Avon struggled on, becoming unnavigable above Pershore in the 1940s; by 1949 it looked as if all was lost.

Then things changed. C. D. Barwell bought the Lower Avon Navigation Company and formed the Lower Avon Navigation Trust 'to improve and maintain the navigation'. Locks and weirs were rebuilt, restored and repaired—two unfortunate casualties were the Cropthorne and Pershore watergates, two of the last of the flashlocks—and the navigation was reopened to Evesham in 1961. The cost—£100,000—was raised from private sources with no government assistance.

A few years later the Upper Avon Trust was formed and David Hutchings, well known for his work on the restoration of the Stratford Canal, was put in charge. Restoration work began in 1968, involving the construction of nine locks and lowering the foundations of an arch of Bidford bridge. Stratford lock itself, with its overhead bracing girders, is now one of the tourist sights of the town. Here and there you can find old Thames Conservancy paddle gear, with its spoked wheel, now adapted to opening lock gates. Weir Brake lock, the last to be completed, was finished in thirty-eight working days. It is 110ft long, 23ft wide and about 18ft deep, with sheet metal piled walls and reinforced concrete floor, sills and copings. It cost about £11,000, nearly all of which was for the materials as the Upper Avon labour force was almost wholly voluntary. On 1 June 1974, the navigation was reopened by the Queen Mother.

In general, the lowest lock on a main river marks the boundary between tidal and non-tidal waters. Avon lock at Tewkesbury keeps out the Severn tides, which can be felt as high as Diglis locks, Worcester. On the Trent, the enormous Cromwell lock marks a firm division, the river below it often racing at 5 knots or more. The lowest lock on the Thames, Richmond, is a half tide lock, the effects of the tides between here and Teddington being diminished by the lowering of gates at certain times. On the Great Ouse the tidal waters are cut off at Denver Sluice but affect the upper river by their passage along the straight cut of the New Bedford. This policy—the placing of barriers like Denver across tidal rivers—caused much controversy in earlier times, one engineer describing it as 'barbaric'. But, ultimately, the wisdom of the policy depends on the configuration of the river valley, the risks of flooding, and—though nowadays to a much lesser extent—the needs of the navigation. The Tyne, the Clyde and the Tay, for example, have no barriers; but at the present time the largest barrier of all is being constructed across the estuary of the Thames.

The most recently completed tidal barrage is Barmby at the confluence of the Derwent and the Yorkshire Ouse. This structure has two vertical lifting gates and a navigation lock; by keeping salt water out of the Derwent it enables far more fresh water to be abstracted for

Clunie Dam in the Tummel Valley, Perthshire. Note the fish-ladder on the left of the dam

public supply. The Grand Sluice at Boston, a much older construction, is an automatically operated sea-lock keeping the North Sea tides out of the Witham. On the River Nene is Dog-in-a-Doublet sluice and lock, opened in 1937 and taking its name from the nearby public house. This was built about a hundred years after its construction had first been mooted. It was a major part of the Catchment Board's improvement scheme to control this difficult river in which the levels varied so greatly. Dog-in-a-Doublet has two sluices and a large navigation lock, all with vertically rising gates.

Let us go back and look at the oldest of all these major works, Denver Sluice. This was first built in 1682; it blew up in 1715 and after many years of argument was replaced in 1751. It was again replaced, to the design of Sir John Rennie, in 1834. It has been called 'the key to the drainage of the Fens'; it consists of three sluices, a large vertically rising gate and a navigation lock with two sets of gates so that it can be used whatever the water levels on either side. Within a few hundred yards is the large A. G. Wright sluice on the relief channel; there are also three sluices on the cut-off channel, which swings around the Ouse tributaries taking off the flood water. And nearby is the very much smaller Old Bedford tidal sluice, only usable when the water on each side makes a level; then both sets of gates can be opened for about twenty minutes on the ebb tide, allowing boats to pop in or out as quickly as they can. (See the diagram on page 46.)

Many weirs and smaller dams can be found in our rivers although the reasons for their original construction are no longer clear. Often their purpose was to build up a head of water to power a riverside mill as at Skenfrith on the Monnow where the mill, still working though not water-powered, stands by the wall of the ruined castle. Dams were one of the many interests of the great eighteenth-century civil engineer, John Smeaton; his surviving works include the Larbert and Dunipace dams on the River Carron to supply water power for the many wheels operating at the Carron Ironworks near Falkirk, and a dam on the Coquet, also for an ironworks. Smeaton's instructions for the building of this dam are particularly detailed and complete. 'There is not a more difficult or hazardous piece of work within the compass of civil engineery than the establishment of a high dam upon a rapid river that is liable to great and sudden floods, and such I esteem the river Coquett, and such the dam here proposed to be erected.' With these words he prefaced his instructions, continuing to say that in view of the disasters which might occur 'too much care and circumspection cannot be used in putting the design here proposed into execution'. That both

(*above*) Rutland Water: the dam at the eastern end;

(*below*) Great Barford lock, reconstructed in 1976 as part of the scheme for re-opening the navigation of the Great Ouse to Bedford. The earlier lock was by the landing stage upstream, beside which some of the original lock gear is preserved. Note the protective barrier for the weir on the right. The river was diverted through the field on the left while work was taking place; the old lock was demolished by the voluntary labour of the Waterway Recovery Group, and the Great Ouse Restoration Society made a handsome donation towards the cost of the project

the design and workmanship were up to Smeaton's high standards are shown by the dam's survival for over 200 years.

The Coquet dam was built of rubble masonry, faced with blocks of stone, but the early reservoir dams were made of earth. Several of these were built, some for canal reservoirs and others for water-storage and supply, in the early nineteenth century. Puddled clay formed the centre of the structure; this was covered in earth, grass being sown on the outward face while the water side was faced with masonry. Many of them were built across streams in the Pennines to serve the growing towns and industries of northern England. In 1864 the 95ft high Dale Dyke dam, part of the Sheffield water-supply system, collapsed, and about 200 million gallons of water flooded the valley below, killing 250 people and destroying nearly 800 houses.

The earliest of the great masonry dams in Britain was completed in 1892 on the Afon Vyrnwy in Montgomeryshire where a reservoir—Lake Vyrnwy—was created to supply water to Liverpool. Many more masonry and concrete dams have been built since then, notably in Wales and Scotland, among them the first concrete arch dam at Lake Trawsfynnyd, the 165ft high dam at Loch Sloy and the first pre-stressed concrete dam at Allt-na-Lairige, north of Glasgow. Construction of great reservoirs has often been surrounded by controversy, particularly when Welsh water has been diverted to English towns, when villages have been drowned or areas of great natural beauty or interest have disappeared. Yet the dams themselves and the waters they impound have a majesty and beauty of their own.

Although a reservoir and dam are sited on the course of a waterway, it is often not only that single waterway that provides the supply. Grafham Water is a recent example; constructed in the valley of the Diddington Brook, it obtains much of its water by abstraction from the Great Ouse above Huntingdon. The dam at Grafham is 150ft at the crest and 5,600ft long at water level. When full, the reservoir contains 13,000 million gallons. Yet this is only half the capacity of the latest reservoir, known as Rutland Water as it has submerged a sizable portion of the old county. This lake, on the course of the River Gwash, abstracts from the Welland and the Nene and its surface area is over 3,000 acres. The dam is of clay. It does not, like many dams, dominate the landscape when seen from below, but it is two-thirds of a mile long and no less than half a mile wide at its base. Rutland Water is the largest manmade lake in the country, with a surface area about the same as Lake Windermere. Only time will tell if it will become an accepted part of the countryside, when it has lost its novelty and rawness.

RIVERS IN HISTORY

The names of some of our rivers are among the oldest names we know of in our history. For any study of them, Eilert Ekwall's *English River Names* is indispensable, and there is little purpose in investigating the subject, or in making any useful assessment of the historical importance of rivers, without reference to his findings. The first part of this chapter, then, is a tribute to the work of this Swedish scholar, without which we might well make unfounded assumptions or ridiculous mistakes.

The older river-names date from before the Anglo-Saxon invasions; examples include Thames, Medway, Colne, Stour, Wey, Kennet, Avon, Axe, Dart, Severn, Ouse, Trent, Nene, Welland, Dee, Don, Wharfe, Derwent, Tees, Tyne, Tame, Lune, Duddon and Esk. Next in time come Old English names like Swale, Bourne, Fleet, Cherwell, Ray, Blackwater, Hamble, Ebble, Otter, Salwarpe, Blyth, Manifold, Mersey and Irwell. In some counties, Scandinavian names are found, such as Wreak, Bain, Skerne, Greta, Rothay and Borrow. There are also several back-formations, where the name of a river comes, consciously or subconsciously, from the name of a place or a person connected with it. Among back-formations are Cuckmere, Arun, Adur, Roding, Crouch, Chelmer, Ver, Mole, Wandle, Evenlode, Pang, Chelt, Deben, Lark, Bure, Nar and Eamont.

Some of the early names are descriptive: Cam, Weaver and Wheelock all mean 'winding', Leadon is 'broad', Lugg, Nidd and Perry are 'white' or 'bright', Dove is 'dark' or 'black', Carant is 'friendly'. Some derive from names of trees or plants, such as Derwent and Dart (oak), Cole (hazel), Wearne (elder), Iwerne (yew) and Corse (reed), and a few from names of animals, like Ock (salmon) and Yarty (bear). A great many names mean simply 'river', 'water' or 'stream', including Avon, Dore, Goyt, Esk and its variants, Don, Ouse and Nadder. Often these are rivers of some size—'the river' of the locality. And sometimes the

Frontispiece from Samuel Ireland's *Picturesque Views on the River Medway*, 1793. He wrote: 'The original design of the annexed frontispiece is from the skilful hand of his late ingenious friend, John Mortimer. It applied so happily to the fine poetical imagery of our bard Spenser on the supposed marriage of the THAMES and MEDWAY, as to leave the author almost in doubt; whether when the sketch was made, the Painter had not an eye to the Poet'

use of such a name may be an indication of river-worship at some period, the older, sacred name having become taboo and being replaced in everyday use by a word meaning simply 'river' or something general and unspecific. Moreover we should not forget that people living near to a river today often simply refer to it as 'the river'; so might the Britons have called their river Afon (Avon) and the Saxons have called theirs 'Bourne'.

Names of British rivers provide some evidence of river-worship, but to nothing like the extent taken by this form of belief in ancient Greece. In Greece, according to Hesiod, there were 3,000 rivers, the divine sons of Oceanus and Tethys. They were depicted as strong, two-horned men with flowing beards. Achelous was the most celebrated Greek river-god, with six rivers named after him; one of his horns was torn off by Hercules and was turned by the water-nymphs into the Horn of Plenty. In addition, the streams, brooks and pools each had their own nymph, generally benevolent but not immortal—Plutarch put the nymphs' average life-span at 9,620 years.

In Britain the name Dee, originating from Deua or Deva, means 'goddess'; in all probability 'goddess of war' as the alternative Welsh name Aerfen has this meaning. As a border river for much of its course, the North Wales and Cheshire Dee had a special significance; the Druids and the Christian Britons regarded it as holy, and even in the nineteenth century Tennyson refers to it as 'sacred'. Edgar, King of England from 959 to 975, was rowed up the Dee in his royal barge by four kings and founded the great church at Chester, or so it was said.

A much less notable river, the Brent, derives its name from the Old British Brigantia. She was a goddess; the river itself may have been named directly after her, or its name may mean the exalted or holy river. Brigantia symbolised abundance; she became transmuted into the St Brigid of Ireland and sorts oddly today with the Northern Line tube station of Brent Cross, between Hendon Central and Golders Green on the London Underground.

It is very likely that the names of the Rivers Kent, Kennet and Kennett are identical in origin: the etymology indicates a stem with the meaning 'high'. The latter two rivers do not run through high country, and the 'high' is more probably metaphorical, with the sense of holy or exalted. The name Lune—there are two River Lunes, the well known one in Lancashire and the shorter tributary of the Tees in Yorkshire—may mean 'health-giving' and again there is an implication of river-worship. The various Rivers Aln, Allan and Allen can also be connected with the meaning 'holy'. Etymologists, however, are not notable for agreeing with each other and to look much further in nomenclature for evidence of river-worship is to venture upon shaky ground, perhaps to fall into a quagmire—or into the River Waveney which, etymologically, may be the same thing. But no matter how shaky this ground, it is more secure than that on which charming but unscholarly authorities asserted that the Trent was so named because it had thirty tributaries or types of fish in its waters, or that the Mole was so called because it behaved like one.

The use of the word 'devil' in the name of a river or stream—Devil's Brook or Devil's Water are examples—seems originally to have had nothing to do with the Old Boy himself. Such names, and others including Divelish, Dulas and the better-known Douglas, have the meaning of 'dark' or 'black' and there is no reason to connect them with devil-worship nor is there any proof of association with evil or fear. The darkness or blackness refers to the apparent colour of the water or to the darkness of the bed over which it runs. Far more ominous is the name of a Northumberland stream, the Wreigh Burn, a tributary of the Coquet. This is 'the stream in which felons were drowned', referring to an ancient custom of execution by drowning. In Lincolnshire, the name of the Waring, a tributary of the Bain, carries the same meaning. With his hands tied under his legs, the criminal was thrown into the stream; perhaps a temporary dam would be made to deepen the water. Ekwall notes that the Wreigh Burn flows near Rothbury and the Waring through Horncastle, both towns long established as judicial centres. Another method of execution by water was by tying the victim to a stake in an estuary at low tide, or to the piers of a bridge in a tidal river. The corpse would be left for several days as a warning. Trial by water was one of the methods used for the detection of witches, though more often a pond was used than a river. If the suspect floated it proved she was a witch; if she sank then she wasn't—a case of heads I win, tails you lose.

Some river-names have a magic, a music of their own that has more to do with poetry than with etymology. Evenlode, Windrush and Medway, for example, or Derwent, Harbourne and Rivelin. Ekwall tells us that Evenlode is named after the village so called, Windrush may mean 'white or happy flowing' and Medway is a compound which could mean 'the river with sweet or honey-coloured water'. Note the cautionary verbs 'may' and 'could'. The meanings notwithstanding, few would deny the music of the names.

As might be expected, some river-names mean no more than 'boundary'. One such is Sheaf, a tributary of the Don, which for some of its short distance marks the boundary between Derbyshire and

Yorkshire; in pre-Conquest times this was the boundary between Mercia and Northumbria. Across the other side of the country, the River Parrett was the dividing line between the Belgic and Danmonian tribes. In the settlement made between King Alfred and Guthrum, the Thames, Ouse and Trent were the chief lines of demarcation. The Trent has served—and still serves—as a boundary in many different ways. Remains of many hill forts of the Iron Age have been found on its northern side. Before the Roman invasion it divided British tribes, and it was the limit of the Roman advance in the first century AD. Later the Romans treated it as part of a trade route; then the invaders from Scandinavia used it to penetrate deep into England. At one time it formed a barrier between the earldoms of Leofric and Beorn, and in the Civil War the Trent Valley was a broad division between the Parliamentarians to the south and the Royalists to the north. It has been said of the Trent, in a slightly different connection, that 'when a hole is dug deeply enough it produces white gypsum on one bank of the river and black coal on the other'.

The Mersey is another important boundary river; it is likely that this is the meaning of its name. The river was the boundary between Mercia and Northumbria and it was fortified in at least three places by Edward the Elder in the tenth century. Until the cutting of the Manchester Ship Canal, the Mersey was part of the boundary between Cheshire and Lancashire; since then, when the canal took over this role, it has divided the dioceses of Chester and Liverpool. But the river was not only a barrier; as Warrington, the lowest crossing point, developed, it became a distribution centre for the men of the Bronze Age, who made their goods in Ireland and shipped them over to Warrington, whence they were distributed on both sides of the river, in Cheshire and Lancashire. Much later, King John founded the borough of Liverpool, protected by a castle, to provide a port for Ireland, free from the influence of the Earl of Chester. For about 400 years the small port remained stable and secure, growing little, with its citizens inhabiting seven short streets. Then the West Indian trade began and, with it, the period of growth until, from Liverpool, ships sailed for South Africa, South America and the Far East.

Some rivers are ancient barriers between peoples and tribes, as the Severn was between the Saxons and the Celts. Many of the old barriers survive as county boundaries. At Newbridge there used to be a scampering across the Thames from the Maybush in Berkshire to the Rose Revived in Oxfordshire at 10 o'clock when the Berkshire pubs closed half an hour earlier than the Oxfordshire houses. The Dove forms part of the boundary between Derbyshire and Staffordshire; 'I am glad to see you safe over,' says Piscator; 'and now you are welcome into Staffordshire.'

'How, Staffordshire?' remarks Viator, in some surprise. 'What do I there, trow? there is not a word of Staffordshire in all my direction.'

'You see,' replies Piscator, 'you are betrayed into it . . .' and often we are still betrayed into another county by the crossing of a bridge.

Perhaps of all the county boundaries, the Tamar is the strongest defined. For most of its length it cuts off Cornwall from Devon and the rest of England and there are still comparatively few bridges across it. Yet the Tamar gives a unique character to its valley and, until the railway age, it was the principal highway for a great part of it. In one sense it divided, in another it united. With so many rivers it is the same; they appear to be barriers but they are also, and often far more significantly, a series of links. Our rivers are not so wide nor so fierce that fording, ferrying or bridging became impossibilities or so difficult or dangerous as to be deterrents. With the steep banks and infrequent bridges on the Tamar, it was the ferry crossings that united the region and brought prosperity to it.

The river barriers, then, were not insurmountable. When a really tough barrier was needed it was specially built—Hadrian's Wall and Offa's Dyke are well known examples. Both stride across the countryside where the strategists felt they were most needed; neither simply reinforced the line of a river. For to be used as a frontier it had to be defended by strongholds; during the Danish invasion, the Thames formed part of the frontiers of Wessex, and Oxford, where the Cherwell meets the Thames, was the chief of these, founded by Edward the Elder about AD 912.

By the Thames, and by many other rivers, early ecclesiastical settlements were founded and grew up. Sometimes the river was the highway along which stone for the building was brought. Norwich priory and cathedral were built of stone from Normandy, iron from Sweden and Baltic timber, transhipped at Yarmouth and brought along the Yare and Wensum, finishing their journey by a canal cut from the Wensum at Pull's Ferry. At Rievaulx, canals were cut from the River Rye for the transportation of stone from quarries nearby to the site of the buildings. There were abbeys at Tewkesbury, Pershore and Evesham by the Avon, Rochester was served by the Medway and the religious foundations of Canterbury by the Kentish Stour. One of the most beautifully sited of religious houses, although it was by no means a wealthy foundation, was Tintern Abbey on the banks of the Wye. By or near to the Severn were built Buildwas Abbey and the cathedrals of Worcester and Gloucester. Peterborough Cathedral is within a few hundred yards of the Nene and Durham Cathedral overlooks the Wear; indeed, it is difficult to find any important religious foundation that is not situated within easy reach of a river of some significance. Look to the north east, for example, to Northumberland and the Border counties of Scotland. In a curve of the Coquet are the remains of Brinkburn Priory. The deep sound of its bell is said to have betrayed the position of the priory to the marauding Scots, seeking it in the woodlands that once filled the Coquet valley. They discovered the priory and attacked it, and either they or the surviving monks threw the bells into the river where—for all anyone knows to the contrary—they may still be.

By the River Aln are the ruins of Hulne Priory, which rivals Aylesford on the distant Medway as the first Carmelite house to be founded in England. North of the Border are the beautiful remains of Jedburgh, near the clear Jed Water that joins the Teviot south of Roxburgh. Nothing remains of Roxburgh convent, and very little of its castle, but by the Tweed are the ruins of Kelso and, to the west, the more impressive remains of the two other great Scottish Border abbeys, Dryburgh and Melrose. Then come southwards, back across the Border to the valley of the Irthing, a tributary of the Eden, and to Lanercost Priory, many of whose stones came from the Roman Wall.

So in their verdant river valleys the various ecclesiastical foundations prospered—or failed to prosper—in their different ways. The abbots and abbesses often owned mills and fisheries. Bridges were built and marshes were drained by the monks of old. Fountains Abbey was built beside—and parts of it above—the River Skell, which provided the community with fresh water and carried away the waste and sewage. A supply of fresh running water was essential for the great monastic houses and if nature did not provide it then streams had to be diverted or canals to be cut. Over such a stream or drain would be the necessarium, where monastic backsides were suspended at appropriate times. Sometimes the necessarium would be divided by partitions, but at Furness there was a long double row of seats, back to back. Many of the great religious houses have survived the vicissitudes of time and, though usually much rebuilt and restored, continue today as the cathedrals, abbeys and priories of the Church of England. Of others—Crowland near the Welland in Lincolnshire or Abbey Dore in the Golden Valley of the Dore in Herefordshire—parts are still in use but the greater glories have been destroyed. The west end of Llanthony Priory by the Honddu in Monmouthshire has become a hotel. Forde Abbey, by the Axe in

163

Tintern Abbey on the Wye, from a nineteenth-century engraving

Dorset, is now a private house of some splendour; Lacock Abbey, near the Wiltshire Avon, belongs to the National Trust, and Newstead Abbey, of the Augustinian order, founded in 1170 by Henry II, after the dissolution of the monasteries was converted into the family home of the Byrons. With its lake and waterfalls it stands by the River Leen.

The ruins and remains of many other great institutions, Fountains, Rievaulx and Tintern among them, are now in the care of the Department of the Environment, the ivy stripped from their crumbling walls, their lawns well-manicured and their charges for admission increasing, it seems, every year. And a few, like Eynsham on the upper Thames in Oxfordshire, have disappeared almost entirely, though stones from their fabric have been used in buildings nearby.

From riverside sites Christianity spread throughout the kingdom and by river banks and crossings decisive battles were fought. Except in a geological sense, a river cannot really be said to have a history of its own; you can trace, say, the history of its navigation but not the history of the river itself. But because they are frontiers or barriers, because their crossings form nodal points, because major towns and ports grow up around the lowest crossing of a tidal river, because of their various functions—power, fertilisation, drainage—much that is significant in history happens on their banks.

Unlike their English counterparts, the great rivers of Scotland—Forth, Clyde, Tay, Dee and Spey—were impossible for navigation more than a few miles from the sea. It has been well said that the great waterway of pre-industrial Scotland was the sea; the estuaries of Clyde, Forth and Tay cut deeply into Scotland and most of the larger towns that were not actually on the coast were accessible to sea-going ships. The few canals that were cut in Scotland joined sea, estuaries or lochs; no network like that in the midland counties of England was envisaged or constructed. The Scottish rivers, then, have no navigation history to compare with that of the Thames, Severn, Trent or the other major English water routes.

But a look at the course of one of the great Scottish rivers—the Dee, for example—brings to mind names and events that ring and echo through history. 'The infant rills of Highland Dee', according to James Hogg, are guarded by 'grisly cliffs ... where hunter's horn is never heard'. The river descends from its source on Braeriach, the highest source of any river in the country. Some 20 miles on, when the river has left the bleak and misty heights, it comes to the first of the tourist haunts, the Linn of Dee. Here, where the old bridge was swept away by floods in 1829, the water is contracted through a narrow cleft in the rocks. 'One may descend to the river's edge,' in the words of Black's *Picturesque Tourist of Scotland*, 'and the furious mass of waters, crushed and huddled together by the impregnable stone walls, raves with a wild and deafening fury, that dizzies the brain, and excites a sort of apprehension that the exasperated element may leap from its prison, and overwhelm the spectator as he is coolly gazing on its agony. It is easy to step from the north bank to the south; but the adventurer should adopt the old counsel of looking before leaping.' This is where Lord Byron, as a boy, nearly fell in, and where a new granite bridge was opened by Queen Victoria in 1857.

On the upper Dee are Invercauld Castle and Braemar; Kenneth II, King of Scotland from 971 to 995, hunted here and Malcolm Canmore, the last of the Celtic kings of Scotland, built a castle in the forest. In 1715 the eleventh Earl of Mar, John Erskine, set up here the standard of rebellion that was intended to restore James, the Old Pretender, to the throne. Now Braemar sees the annual gathering of the clans, and the hotels and boarding houses are full of tourists.

Between Braemar and Ballater on the south bank of the Dee is the castle of Balmoral, an essential ingredient in the chronicles of royalty over the last 130 years. Here has been a castle since at least 1452; later it had a close association with the Jacobite rebellions. After the '45 it was bought by the Earl of Fife. Victoria and Albert visited it in 1847 and, five years later, Albert completed the purchase of the estate. A new castle was built, in the very epitome of the style of Scottish Baronial, with tartan and draughts everywhere. It was Victoria's favourite home, and all her successors—with the understandable exception of her son—have used and enjoyed it.

The royal favour accorded to Balmoral has encouraged the development of Deeside as a playground for the wealthy and an attraction for the holidaymaker. Ballater was the terminus of the Deeside Extension Railway (by royal insistence) and now is a village of boarding houses and a caravan park. A mile or so away is the place where, some 400 years ago, Gordon, Lord of Brackley, was killed by Farquharson of Inverey. Farquharson had many men with him and Gordon knew he stood no chance; but his beautiful, unfaithful wife accused him of cowardice. 'There's a Gordon rides out that will never ride hame', he said, as he kissed her farewell; and he never did.

Nearby, on the north bank of the river are the ruins of Tullich kirk, where St Nathalan's chapel once stood. This saint, believing himself guilty of some great (but unspecified) sin, locked an iron chain around his waist and threw the key into a pool in the river. Later, on a pilgrimage to Rome he was given a fish, in whose belly was the key; so

Invercauld Bridge—Brig O'Dee—over the Dee, built in 1752

he knew he was forgiven. Tullich kirk is said to have been where the Highland reel of Tullochgorum originated when the congregation, awaiting in vain a belated minister one wintry morning, began to dance and drink to keep themselves warm. By the end of the year, it is said, they were all dead.

Heading downriver we come to a tributary, the Tanar, flowing through the remnants of the old Caledonian Forest, and the castle of Aboyne, ancestral home of the Gordons, whose chief is known as the Cock o'the North. There are, among others, the castles of Crathes, Tilquhillie and Drum, the latter dating in part from the thirteenth century and still the home of the Irvines as it was when first built. Then there is Aberdeen and the old Bridge of Dee, built in the 1520s, with its coats of arms and inscriptions. Once it had a chapel and a defensive gateway, both now disappeared. It was the scene of a two-day battle in 1639, when the Covenanters, under the command of Montrose, defeated the supporters of King Charles, led by Lord Aboyne, and occupied the town.

Many reaches of the Dee are associated with Lord Byron—it is hard, but not impossible, to avoid quotation. Similarly much of the Forth is associated with Sir Walter Scott, and the Tay with William McGonagall. Literature aside, the Forth is the river of greatest importance in Scottish history. 'Half the important events in Scottish annals have taken place on or near the banks of the river, and of the Firth,' wrote John Geddie. Until recent times, the first bridge over the Forth has been at Stirling, overlooked by a castle dominating the plain. Seven historic battles were fought within sight of the castle rock: Cambuskenneth, Stirling, Falkirk, Bannockburn, Sauchieburn, Sherriffmuir and, again, Falkirk, the earliest between the Picts and the Scots in AD 843, and the last in 1746, when the Young Pretender won a battle but failed to take Stirling Castle and went on to lose a war.

No English river can be thought of as the key to a kingdom in the same way that one can regard the Forth in Scottish history. In the context of history, however, the Thames is the richest of our rivers. The upper Thames was disputed between Mercia and Wessex; Alfred held a parliament at Shifford; Henry IV lost a battle at Radcot; Oxford was the Royalist headquarters in the Civil War; eleven of our monarchs are buried at Windsor and King John put his seal to Magna Carta in the meadow at Runnymede. On the way to London is the site of Chertsey Abbey; then come the palaces of Hampton Court, Westminster, Somerset House, Greenwich and Tilbury Fort. Historians, painters, poets have immortalised the lot. On 3 September 1803, Wordsworth composed a sonnet upon Westminster Bridge. 'Earth has not any thing to shew more fair,' he began, and in the very early morning, when 'all that mighty heart is lying still', many people would agree with him. Forty years before—to shift the viewpoint a little—another famous writer had used the same bridge for a rather different purpose. It was on a Tuesday, in May 1763, when James Boswell had dined with a friend and then gone on to Lord Eglington's. But his lordship was late and Boswell, tired of waiting, left. 'At the bottom of the Haymarket,' he wrote, 'I picked up a strong, jolly, young damsel, and taking her under the arm I conducted her to Westminster Bridge, and then in armour complete did I engage her upon this noble edifice. The whim of doing it there with the Thames rolling below us amused me much. Yet'—and here comes his Scottish conscience—'after the brutish appetite was sated, I could not but despise myself for being so closely united with such a low wretch.' Boswell spent several, more innocent, hours being rowed up and down the Thames; 'the silver Thames', he calls it. 'It is very pleasant to sail upon it; and I shall do it oftener.' Drayton wrote about many rivers in *Poly-Olbion*; he also composed an *Ode . . . in the Peake* where

> . . . many Rivers cleare
> Here glide in Silver Swathes.

Tennyson wrote about the Lincolnshire streams and about the Severn up which the body of his friend Henry Hallam was borne on its way to burial. Milton dipped a poetic toe into the Severn and Shakespeare referred to it in *Henry IV*. Hotspur related the story of how Mortimer and Glendower fought hand to hand 'on the gentle Severn's sedgy bank', pausing three times to drink

> Upon agreement, of swift Severn's flood;
> Who then affrighted with their bloody looks
> Ran fearfully among the trembling reeds
> And hid his crisp head in the hollow bank,
> Bloodstained with these valiant combatants.

Not surprisingly, his story failed to impress King Henry. Later in the same play the rebels argue about how to divide the kingdom among themselves and Hotspur complains how the 'smug and silver Trent'.

> . . . comes me cranking in.
> And cuts me from the best of all my land.

168

A futile and inconclusive argument ensues, futile as we know because the rebels are defeated and Hotspur killed. But a look at the map will show the justice of his complaint.

The Trent was also George Eliot's river; in her novel *The Mill on the Floss*, the Floss is the Trent and the town she calls St Ogg's is Gainsborough. The scene is set in the opening sentences of the book.

> A wide plain, where the broadening Floss hurries on between its green banks to the sea, and the loving tide, rushing to meet it, checks its passage with an impetuous embrace. On this mighty tide the black ships—laden with the fresh-scented fir-planks, with rounded sacks of oil-bearing seed, or with the dark glitter of coal—are borne along to the town of St Ogg's, which shows its aged, fluted red roofs and the broad gables of its wharves between the low wooded hill and the river-brink, tinging the water with a soft purple hue under the transient glance of this February sun . . . Just by the red-roofed town the tributary Ripple flows with a lively current into the Floss.

George Eliot's Ripple is an imaginary tributary of the Trent, based perhaps on one of the Warwickshire streams she knew when she was young. It is in the flooded Trent that Maggie and Tom Tulliver drown at the end of the book.

Dickens is the great novelist of the Thames, particularly the tidal reaches. Time and again he returns to the river—in *The Old Curiosity Shop, Great Expectations, Our Mutual Friend*. Usually it is the more macabre aspects that attract him. 'The very fire that warmed you when you were a babby, was picked out of the river alongside the coal barges,' Gaffer Hexam tells his daughter Lizzie. 'The very basket that you slept in, the tide washed ashore. The very rockers that I put it upon to make a cradle of it, I cut out of a piece of wood that drifted from some ship or other.' There is a grislier side to Hexam's activities. He sees no wrong in robbing a corpse, and it is for the bodies of drowned men that he searches, with Lizzie at the oars. As they pull for home, 'what he had in tow lunged itself at him sometimes in an awful manner when the boat was checked, and sometimes seemed to try to wrench itself away, though for the most part it followed submissively'. Yet in this great novel, *Our Mutual Friend*, the river is symbolic. It is the river of life and the river of death. In Plashwater Mill Weir Lock, Bradley Headstone and Rogue Riderhood both drown, and from that same reach of the Thames, some 25 miles upstream from London, Lizzie rescues Eugene Wrayburn, after Headstone's attempt to murder him, and nurses him back to health, a new view of life, and happiness in marriage.

169

Greta Bridge, 1977. The bridge was built by Sir Walter Scott's friend,
Mr Morritt owner of the Rokeby estate, in 1789, replacing an older
one. It is bypassed now, and used only by light traffic

The Greta, a tributary of the Tees, has been immortalised in quite
different ways by Dickens and by Sir Walter Scott. Scott expatiated upon
its beauties in both verse and prose; for Dickens, the George and New
Inn at Greta Bridge was the place where Nicholas Nickleby, Mr Squeers,
the little boys and their luggage were deposited on their way to
Dotheboys Hall, whose original was in the village of Bowes, 4 miles
away. Also in the north the Yarrow has been poetised and Tweed and
Till have their ominous, anonymous rhyme. Far away in the South
West, the Dart echoes the dangers of the Till:

> River Dart, oh River Dart,
> Every year thou claimest a heart!

In different mood and tempo, William McGonagall wrote about the
fair city of Glasgow,

> Where the river Clyde rolls on to the sea,
> And the lark and the blackbird whistle with glee.

170

The silvery Tay, however, was McGonagall's favourite river, with its new railway bridge and its side-screens:

> Which will be a great protection on a windy day,
> So as the railway carriages won't be blown away,
> And ought to cheer the hearts of the passengers night and day
> As they are conveyed along thy beautiful railway,
> And towering above the silvery Tay,
> Spanning the beautiful river shore to shore
> Upwards of two miles and more . . .

Now look, if only briefly, at the relationship between painters and some of our rivers. Again, the Thames has provided, as might be expected, the chief source of inspiration. Artists from abroad—Canaletto, Monet, Derain—have painted the London Thames in its varying moods, with the great riverside buildings, such as Somerset House, Greenwich Hospital and Barry's Houses of Parliament. 'Along with the Seine,' said Geoffrey Grigson, 'the Thames after all turns out to be the most painted river in Europe,' though most of the painters who came over from the Low Countries or France did not get further upstream than Richmond. Rubens put the Thames and a collection of London landmarks into the background of his *Landscape with St George and the Dragon*, which portrayed Charles I as St George rescuing Henrietta Maria before a numerous, and not surprisingly rather flabbergasted-looking, audience in varying stages of disarray. Hondius painted the frozen Thames with old London Bridge and old St Paul's; Jan Siberichts got as far upriver as Henley and also painted an expansive rural view of Nottingham and the Trent at the end of the seventeenth century. Canaletto's better English scenes were of Thameside London, but he did paint a detailed study of the wooden bridge over the river at Walton, a mathematical structure that lasted only two years. Corot painted the Thames at Richmond, but the French painter most devoted to the Thames, its bridges and buildings, was Claude Monet. Monet painted nearly a hundred pictures of London, most of them depicting the Thames. In his dedication to the river he rivalled the American-born James McNeill Whistler who lived near the Thames and portrayed it in oils, etchings and lithographs for over forty years.

None of the greater British painters of landscape showed the same obsession with London's river as Monet or Whistler. Richard Wilson was one of the first of our major landscape artists. Born and brought up in Wales, he travelled extensively in Italy and many of his pictures of

English and Welsh scenes show an Italian influence. One such is his *Holt Bridge on the River Dee*, in the Tate Gallery, a lovely composition but by no means an accurate topographical study. He painted scenes on the Wye and on many Welsh rivers, being one among many artists attracted by the dramatic curve of Edwards's bridge at Pontypridd. One of the most pleasing pastoral views of the Thames, *The Thames near Marble Hill*, he completed about 1762; this is in a more English style and we can clearly recognise the scene today.

The Derbyshire rivers provided popular subjects for a number of artists. Joseph Wright painted the ruins of Dale Abbey beside the Derwent; Dovedale and a night study of Arkwright's cotton mills were among his other major pictures. John Linnell made watercolours and drawings for Walton's *The Compleat Angler*, many of them of the River Dove. And Philip de Loutherbourg, although not an English-born artist, painted a dramatic oil of Dovedale in 1784. This was made following his second visit to Derbyshire; on a previous tour he had made several studies for a pantomime, *The Wonders of Derbyshire*, produced at Drury Lane in 1779. The plot of this pantomime 'was simply developed as a pretext for a number of changes of scenery', which was so constructed as to sweep across the stage in a continuous curve. De Loutherbourg also painted in the Lake District and in Shropshire; his *Coalbrookdale by Night* is one of the best known pictures of the early days of the Industrial Revolution.

The Greta of Dickens and Scott also gave inspiration to the painter John Sell Cotman, who stayed at Rokeby Hall during 1805. His cool and harmonious *Greta Bridge* has been described as 'that loveliest of water-colours'; he was fascinated by the wooded countryside of the meeting of the waters of Greta and Tees and by the shapes and colours of the rocks in the river. Higher up the Tees, Thomas Smith of Derby, one of several artists of the late eighteenth and early nineteenth centuries who toured the country producing paintings and drawings for publication as engravings, visited the waterfall of High Force, of which he made an etching for his *Book of Landskips*. Smith was one among many visitors to the cliffs and waterfalls of Gordale Scar, along with Edward Dayes, Thomas Girtin, Turner and James Ward whose great oil painting brings the strength of the Yorkshire scene into the Tate Gallery.

The Tyne was painted by Thomas Richardson of Newcastle, a fine pastoral scene dominated by a windmill at Gateshead. Linnell painted a tranquil view of the Kennet near Newbury. For those in search of the picturesque, the Lake District and Wales were favourite areas; Thomas Rowlandson's aquatint, *An Artist Travelling in Wales*, makes kindly

James Stark's view of the entrance to Oulton Dyke, connecting Oulton Broad to the Waveney

fun of one such, loaded with impedimenta, mounted on a weak-kneed nag negotiating with difficulty a steep slope down to a valley, and tolerating the downpouring rain with a grim expression and an inadequate umbrella. Many of the estuaries of England, Scotland and Wales were aquatinted by William Daniell for his *Voyage around the Coast of Great Britain*; his *Steam Boat on the Clyde near Dumbarton*, published 1817, is said to be the earliest pictorial representation of such a craft.

The East Anglian painters, of Norwich especially, were particularly concerned with river scenes. John Crome painted and drew in the Lake District, on the Wye and elsewhere, but his paintings of the Wensum, the Yare and the minor Norfolk rivers are among his best and most loved. Among other Norwich artists, John Thirtle, the two sons of Cotman, the Stannards and James Stark are all notable figures. Stark's illustrations of the Norfolk rivers, of which engravings were published in 1834 to mark the opening of the Norwich & Lowestoft Navigation, are a carefully detailed record of the rivers, their scenery, shipping and

Okehampton on the River Okement, drawn and engraved by
F. C. Lewis, 1843

activities of the period. Notable illustrated books of other rivers include
Samuel Ireland's volumes on the Thames, Medway, Wye, Avon and
Severn, F. C. Lewis's engravings of the Devonshire rivers, Wood's *Rivers
of Wales*, Boydell's *Thames*, with aquatints by Farington and Stothard,
and the well known views of the same river by Cooke, Westall and
Tombleson.

Finally there are the three major painters, Gainsborough, Turner and
Constable. Gainsborough preferred landscapes to riverscapes; usually
when rivers appear in his paintings they are incidental to a major theme.
Turner for much of his life lived by the Thames and was continually
fascinated by the interaction of water and light. He painted many

studies of the river, including several near Walton Bridge and the great *England: Richmond Hill, on the Prince Regent's Birthday*, his largest single work. But he travelled all over the country in search of subjects; his pictures show the Tyne, the Tweed, the Lakes, the Yorkshire rivers, the Teign, the Chichester Canal. *Crossing the Brook*, now in the Tate, is a painting, in the manner of Claude, of the Tamar Valley. There are oils and watercolours of the Falls of Clyde, quite different in vision and approach. And one of his later and best-known pictures shows the *Fighting Temeraire* being towed to her final berth on the Thames near Rotherhithe, to be broken up.

The painter most closely identified with a single river is, of course, Constable. His father owned the mills at Flatford and Dedham; John, the fourth child, was born at East Bergholt House. He describes the fertile valley of the Stour, dividing Suffolk from Essex, in the introduction to *English Landscape*, his book of mezzotints: 'The beauty of the surrounding scenery, the gentle declivities, the luxuriant meadow flats sprinkled with flocks and herds, and well cultivated uplands, the woods and rivers, the numerous scattered villages and churches, with farms and picturesque cottages, all impart to this particular spot an amenity and elegance hardly anywhere else to be found.' Much of it is there in the early unfinished painting *The Valley of the Stour*. He travelled around England, learnt more, experienced more and achieved mastery in the techniques of oil painting. In his maturity he painted several large canvases showing scenes on the Stour: *The White Horse, Stratford Mill* (later known as *The Young Waltonians*), *The Hay Wain*—the best-known and most often reproduced of all, yet unsold at its first showing—*View on the Stour, near Dedham, A Boat passing a Lock* and *The Leaping Horse*. Constable painted many scenes other than those beside the Stour, but these river paintings are among the greatest of all. Let his own words, in a letter to John Fisher, end the chapter:

How much I can Imagine myself with you on your fishing excursion in the new forest, what River can it be. But the sound of water escaping from Mill dams delights me, so do Willows, Old rotten banks, slimy posts, & brickwork. I love such things . . . As long as I do paint I shall never cease to paint such Places. They have always been my delight—& I should indeed have been delighted in seeing what you described in your company . . .

But I should paint my own places best—Painting is but another word for feeling. I associate my 'careless boyhood' to all that lies on the banks of the *Stour*. They made me a painter (& I am grateful) that is I had often thought of pictures of them before I had ever touched a pencil.

9

CURIOUS, LOST AND ODD

Most rivers have a clearly recognisable pattern; they do what is expected according to the terrain through which they flow. But there are a few exceptions, of which the Mole in Surrey is one of the best known. Edmund Spenser wrote of this river, 'that like a Mousling mole doth make His way still underground'. Sadly, the river's name is not connected with the rodent although it does at times disappear underground and travellers have been continually fascinated by it.

On John Norden's map of Surrey, drawn in the late sixteenth century, the Mole is shown as far as Dorking. No course of the river is shown for the next 3 miles; instead, the words 'The river goeth underground' fill the gap until it reappears at Norbury. It still does, in the dry periods of some years, disappear underground, falling through several fissures—known as swallow-holes—in the chalk. The fissures in the actual bed of the river can absorb 30 million gallons of water a day and when the flow is less than that the whole course of the river can be sucked into the chalk, to reappear as springs near Leatherhead. Camden, the antiquarian, reported that someone once forced a duck into one of the swallows 'which came out at the other side by Molesey with its feathers almost all rubbed off'. So notorious was the river's behaviour that Defoe gave three pages to it, commenting on those who had written about it without having seen it, describing the scene 'as if the water had at once engulfed itself in a chasm of the earth, or sunk in a whirlpit, as is said of the Caspian Sea, which they say rises again in the Persian Gulph with the same violence that it engulfs itself'. As a result of such accounts, he said, many people visited the area 'not doubting that they should see some wonderful gulf, in which a whole river should be at once as it were buried alive'. Defoe had seen the Mole several times and describes the water gradually sinking into the ground and gradually reappearing; he never saw the channel completely dry.

'Sullen Mole that hides his diving flood', as Pope wrote, was never a navigation, has no towpath and has very few settlements on or near its banks. Near to London and yet remote, the Mole Valley has attracted writers of different kinds over the centuries; Fanny Burney, Sheridan and George Meredith all lived there at one time or another, Keats, Wordsworth, Coleridge and Robert Louis Stevenson were among the many visitors, and Matthew Arnold, towards the end of his life, called himself 'the hermit of the Mole' in a letter written from his cottage at Painshill by the river. It is a beautiful valley, overlooked by Box Hill, with fine country houses and cottages. One of the few villages by the river is Mickleham; it was here, one night in February 1940, that strange rumbling sounds were heard. After finishing his breakfast, the local postman went outside to see what was going on. He noticed a large oak tree swaying about; suddenly it sank straight down into the earth, leaving a large crater full of water. When he peered over the edge he could see the topmost branches of the tree some 15ft below the level of the soil where once the trunk had stood. The theory is that it was the waters of the river, working away underground, that had carried away the soil until there was nothing to support the tree beneath.

The Mole is only one of many rivers that at times disappear underground along part of their course. The valley of one small river in Kent, the Nailbourne, is more often dry than wet, but after heavy rain it can rise and run, to flood the surrounding countryside. Some of these rivers have their own generic names according to their part of the country; in the south they are called 'bournes', in Sussex 'lavants' and in Yorkshire 'gipseys'. In the limestone country of Derbyshire there are some well known examples. On the west side of Dovedale is the valley of the Manifold; near Thor's Cave the river disappears at times through fissures in the limestone for about 4 miles, reappearing near Ilam Hall. This is usually a summertime phenomenon; when there is sufficient flow and the level of the water-table is high enough the river runs as one would expect from the continuous blue line on the map. As with the Mole, when the flow of the river vanishes, pools and puddles remain stagnant on the riverbed. A tributary of the Manifold, the Hamps, disappears in a similar way through fissures in the limestone with the local name of 'shack-holes'. Rising in the hills near Feltysitch, the Hamps runs southwards for a few miles then takes a sharp U-turn to flow north to join the Manifold below Beeston Tor. The Hamps—its name, according to Ekwall, may mean 'summer-dry'—flows only along its subterranean course during dry weather, sometimes for several weeks. Near Buxton, the Derbyshire Wye also sometimes disappears, vanishing

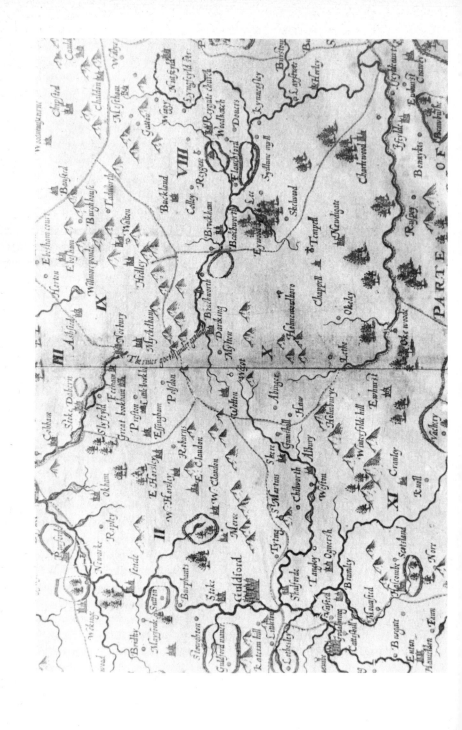

into Plunge Hole, running through Poole's Cave and reappearing at Wye Head.

Vanishing rivers are a characteristic of limestone country. In Yorkshire the Nidd, the Wharfe, the Skirfare and the Aire are among those which in their upper reaches disappear from time to time. Underground caves and tunnels have been carved out by the action of the water. Ingleborough Cave, with its halls and galleries, was once the course of the Clapham Beck and occasionally, in flood-times, part of the beck again runs through it. Fell Beck and its tributaries helped to form the Gaping Gill cave system; the main chamber of Gaping Gill is the largest cave in Britain, 500ft long, 100ft wide and 110ft high. At Malham, the water flowing from the tarn soon disappears, to emerge at the foot of the impressive limestone cliff, Malham Cove, some 300ft high. Disappearing rivers are not, of course, unique to England, but, wherever they are, their effect on the landscape is always fascinating and often dramatic.

Not only natural causes create disappearing rivers. Underneath present-day London there is a large collection of vanished rivers, all of them depicted on early maps. The best-known and largest is the Fleet, with its sources in Highgate and Hampstead joining near Camden Town. It was fed by several wells, St Pancras, Clerkenwell, Bagnigge Wells among them, and was also known as the Hole-bourn and Turnmill Brook. Much of the lower Fleet was navigable; it carried stone for the building of Old St Paul's in the early twelfth century and among other cargoes were corn, wine, firewood, cheese and paving stones, as well as the heavy luggage of the Abbot of Faversham and, sometimes, patients for St Bartholomew's Hospital. It was also used as an open sewer and a linear rubbish dump. Twice in the seventeenth century it is recorded as having to be scoured out as it was impassable.

After the Great Fire of 1666, the lower part of the river, nearly half a mile, was deepened and widened; it was made into a canal, 50ft wide with large wharves and several bridges. Sir Christopher Wren designed a new Holborn bridge at the northern end of the canalised section. Boats used it but it was unremunerative, being subject to silting and too convenient for rubbish disposal. In 1733 it was arched over as far down as Fleet Bridge; the wharves became streets and the canal itself a long covered market. In 1766 the remainder of the canal was covered in; the

(*opposite*) John Norden's map of Surrey, 1595. On the left of the map is the Wey, on the right the Mole, with the disappearing section just to the right of the upper part of the central crease

The River Fleet, about 1700, busy with traffic. The bridge is near
Bridewell

market lasted until 1829 when it was taken down and Farringdon Street
put in its place. Three years later it was converted into a proper sewer,
but in the upper reaches raw sewage still drained directly into what was
an open ditch. It was a source of disease until Sir Joseph Bazalgette's
metropolitan sewage scheme solved the problem, since when it has
served to carry off storm water into the Thames.

Other London rivers include the Westbourne, from Hampstead
through Hyde Park to the Thames at Chelsea; the stretch through the
park was dammed in 1730 and converted into a winding lake—the
Serpentine. The Tyburn has another stream rising near Hampstead. It
flows through the Marylebone area—St Mary-by-the-bourne was the
name of a little church built adjacent to the stream in the sixteenth
century. The Tyburn gave its name to the gallows by Marble Arch;
Tyburn Road and Tyburn Lane were the earlier names of Oxford Street
and Park Lane. Bits of the Tyburn can still be found in unexpected
places; an aqueduct takes it over the Regent's Canal and its waters are
also carried across the District line at Baker Street and Victoria Stations.
The lower course of the Tyburn now flows along a sewer to the Thames.

Some traces of a short river, the Walbrook, have been found during excavations. This ran past the present site of Broad Street Station and under the Bank of England. The church of St Mildred's, in Poultry, was built above the Walbrook. It met the Thames at Dowgate, which was used as a harbour during the Roman occupation.

Among the lesser known tributaries of the London Thames, both of which have disappeared from view, are the Neckinger and the Effra. The Neckinger may have been navigable to Bermondsey Abbey, which built a paper-mill on the stream, later converted to supplying and distributing water to the surrounding area. On the lowest stretch of the Neckinger was St Saviour's Dock. When the watermill was built, various channels were cut; this led to the creation of the district known as Jacob's Island, 'the filthiest, the strangest, the most extraordinary of the many localities that are hidden in London, wholly unknown, even by name, to the great mass of its inhabitants'. So wrote Charles Dickens, in *Oliver Twist*. This was the last refuge of Bill Sikes, an island 'surrounded by a muddy ditch, six or eight feet deep and fifteen or twenty wide when the tide is in, once called Mill Pond, but known in the days of this story as Folly Ditch'. Dickens says that the ditch was filled at high water by the opening of sluices, and goes on to give a vivid account of what happened then:

> At such times, a stranger, looking from one of the wooden bridges thrown across it at Mill Lane, will see the inhabitants of the houses on either side lowering from their back doors and windows, buckets, pails, domestic utensils of all kinds, in which to haul the water up; and when his eye is turned from these operations to the houses themselves, his utmost astonishment will be excited by the scene before him. Crazy wooden galleries common to the backs of half-a-dozen houses, with holes from which to look upon the slime beneath; windows, broken and patched, with poles thrust out, on which to dry the linen that is never there; rooms so small, so filthy, so confined, that the air would seem too tainted even for the dirt and squalor which they shelter; wooden chambers thrusting themselves out above the mud, and threatening to fall into it—as some have done; dirt-besmeared walls and decaying foundations; every repulsive lineament of poverty, every loathsome indication of filth; all these ornament the banks of Folly Ditch.

The area was notorious for cholera; both Dickens and Charles Kingsley testify to the use of what was, in reality, a common sewer as a source of drinking water.

The Effra was a small river south of the Thames, rising in Norwood

(*above*) Another view of the Fleet—too picturesque, probably, to be entirely accurate;
(*below*) the Fleet Ditch in the mid-nineteenth century, at the back of Field Lane. One wonders what the workman is looking for—or has he already found it?

and supplying fresh water to Dulwich into the nineteenth century. It ran by Kennington Church and the Oval—indeed, it was the risk of flooding from the Effra that led to the Oval's preservation as an open space. The Effra is now a storm relief sewer but its name survives in Effra Road and Effra Parade.

There were also the Hackney Brook, a tributary of the Lee, where watercress used to grow, Counter's Creek, the lower two miles of which became in 1828 the Kensington Canal on which a railway line was subsequently built, and Stamford Brook, which had three streams and was the reason for the large number of laundries and breweries in Acton. A full and fascinating account of these and other vanished rivers can be found in Nicholas Barton's book, *Lost Rivers of London*, published in 1962.

The old, vanished London rivers in their time provided routes for navigation, power for watermills and sources of water supply; now for the most part their waters are piped into the Thames, but they are no longer sections of the main sewage lines. Elsewhere in Britain there are few examples of rivers which have been, as it were, obscured by the hand of man. The River Roch does disappear in the centre of Rochdale, but only into a culvert whence it eventually emerges. The Dour, cutting through to the sea at Dover, made possible the haven now the gateway to England, but the little river is mostly culverted through the town. Many rivers, however, have changed their courses, either through natural, geological reasons or as a result of drainage operations. An example of the former is the Kentish Stour, which at one time made the Isle of Thanet a proper island, with connections by fords at Sarre and at St Nicholas at Wade. The channel around the Isle of Thanet used to be called the Wantsum, and the Stour flowed into it at Stourmouth, now some 5 miles inland. The Wantsum is now an insignificant waterway wandering around the marshes of north Kent. In the Middle Ages the Stour was navigable to Fordwich, and, following an Act of 1515, the navigation was extended to Canterbury, although the topmost section of the navigation never appears to have been particularly successful.

At some time Stourmouth ceased to be the mouth of the river, the main channel continuing along, to find its way to the sea at Sandwich. A look at the map shows the strange behaviour of the river as it approaches the sea. It flows eastward to Ebbsfleet, about half a mile from Pegwell Bay; then it turns south, parallel to the coast, to Sandwich, where it turns back on itself to flow north, around Great Stonar, to Pegwell Bay. At Ebbsfleet some notable people have landed in the past, including St Augustine and Hengist and Horsa. As for

Sandwich, one can choose between two descriptions. 'A delightful old town . . . once one of the most important naval bases in England,' says a modern guide-book. 'An old, decayed, poor, miserable town, of which when I have said that it is an ancient town, one of the Cinque Ports, and sends two members to Parliament, I have said all that I think can be worth anybody's reading of the town of Sandwich,' commented Defoe. Any chance that Sandwich could recover its position as a port was ended by the Stonar drainage cut in the late eighteenth century; this joined the two channels of the river south of Ebbsfleet and choked the meander through Sandwich with 'Mud, Sand and Dirt'.

Another river which looks very strange on the map is the Alde. Like the Deben, the Alde has a disproportionately large estuary, the result, it seems, of subsidence in the post-glacial era. The Alde rises near Dennington and makes its way towards the coast via Snape Maltings. East of the Maltings it widens into a marshy estuary; then, just as one would expect it to break through to the sea south of Aldeburgh, it turns sharply south and runs close and parallel to the coast to Orford quay and Havergate Island. Here it is joined by the Butley river, once famous for its oysters, and the combined waters, now known as the River Ore, flow through Orford Haven into the North Sea at Hollesley Bay. In this region, as at better-known Dunwich further north, much has changed and much has gone. Once there was a haven at Thorpe, north of Aldeborough, and a village with docks and quays and a Three Mariners inn at Slaughden. There are photographs of the inn, and in 1900 there were still a handful of inhabited houses at Slaughden. Now there is only a name on the map and a martello tower half a mile to the south.

Indications of shifting coastlines and other geological changes are given by some rivers which rise close to the sea and then flow away from it. In the South West, the Camel, Exe and Torridge behave in this way; so does the Bure in East Anglia, and in the Isle of Wight the Medina and the two River Yars. In Norfolk the Waveney and the Little Ouse rise within a mile of each other and flow in opposite directions. A physical map can explain much that otherwise appears merely contrary or random, but certain phenomena need a knowledge of geology or the history of drainage before they can be understood. The peculiar course of the upper reaches of the Yorkshire Derwent is a case in point. It rises near Filey, quite close to the sea, but its course eastwards was blocked by what geologists call a moraine, a ridge marking the edge of a glacier which, in the so-called Ice Age, came across from Scandinavia. Forced to seek a new outlet, the Derwent flowed inland from the Vale of Pickering through a gorge between the Howardian Hills, on its way capturing the water of the Rye and some other streams before joining the Ouse coming down from York.

Sometimes a straight line in the course of a river indicates a geological fault, the river's natural tendency to wander being checked by a line of weakness in the rock over which it flows. The Vale of Clwyd in North Wales is a good example; in this valley, to use geologists' language, 'the mesozoic rocks lie so enclosed as if in a long bay in the heart of the palaeozoic formations', giving a particular quality to the scenery. But a long straight line more often indicates the hand of man. The name of the waterway itself may be a simple statement of fact; the Middle Level Main Drain, for instance, or the South Forty Foot Drain, or a Dyke or Cut. For the purpose of navigation, some waterways were straightened considerably, not merely by making lock cuts but by constructing lengths of new channel. This is a characteristic of the flatter, eastern half of England, where the Rivers Hull and the Ancholme have two distinct channels for much of their course. The Rivers Aire and Calder were improved into a navigation opened in 1704, and the Calder and the Hebble likewise sixty-six years later.

The courses of the Fenland rivers, especially in their lower reaches, owe far more to the drainage engineer than they do to nature. Aerial photography has revealed much of the older pattern, with the wandering courses of extinct rivers—the West Water and the Welney River are two of them—showing up across the fields. Much of the Welland and its associated waterways is artificial. Most of the Nene below Peterborough is manmade; as well as the leams of Bishop Morton and Humphrey Smith there are Kinderley's Cut, Paupers' Cut—a work to give employment to the poverty-stricken in the early nineteenth century—and the New Outfall Cut, designed by the great engineers Telford and Rennie. And Vermuyden, chief drainer of the Fens, had previously been at work in Hatfield Chase, South Yorkshire, where in the 1630s he cut the Dutch River, at a cost of nearly £30,000, to take the waters of the Don into the Yorkshire Ouse at Goole.

A phenomenon of the behaviour of certain rivers which always creates interest, and can cause danger, is the tidal wave that sweeps up the channel, usually known as the bore or the aegir. This occurs only on a few rivers, notably the Trent, Yorkshire Ouse, Solway Firth, the Parrett and, of course, the Severn. These tidal waves are associated with the funnel shape of estuaries but they are not simply explained by the concentrating of a large volume of water into a narrowing estuary; they do not occur on the Thames, Usk or Clyde, where the estuaries are of similar configuration to those of the rivers where they do occur. Much

185

depends on the flow of water downstream, and it appears that bores occur on rivers whose estuaries are subject to the accumulation of silt and where there is not a constant, heavy flow of fresh water.

On the Severn, the larger bores occur from February to April and August to October. The height of the wave in midstream has been recorded as over 9ft, and the wave reaches a speed of 13mph. More usually the bore is about 3ft high, with some increase on the outer banks of curves. The best place to view the Severn Bore is between Overton and Maisemore, but it can be seen at its most spectacular between Minsterworth and Lower Parting. Riding the bore is exciting and can be dangerous; its frequency on the Severn is one reason why vessels prefer to use the Gloucester & Berkeley Canal. Nevertheless several vessels have used the tidal reaches below Gloucester in recent years, including at least one canal narrow boat, *Heatherbelle*; their skippers have a choice between riding the bore or laying up out of the main channel.

The word 'bore' probably derives from the Scandinavian or Icelandic 'bara', meaning a billow, wave or swell. The alternative name, aegir or eagre, is used on the northern rivers, whereas on the Parrett the tidal wave is more prosaically known as the 'head of tide'. On the Trent one would see not a single crested wave but a succession of steep, rounded waves, sometimes followed by a second instalment, known on the Trent as the 'second shove' and on the Yorkshire Ouse as the 'second swell'. If the first series is large, the second is not so likely to follow. On the Trent the aegir itself can be easily felt at Gainsborough, but the 'second shove' does not reach that far up. The tidal wave can be used to advantage by craft heading upstream; the Trent barges save fuel by following it and the smaller bore on the less-used Parrett was useful to the barge-masters voyaging up through Bridgwater to Langport. The Parrett bore is usually between 2 and 4ft at its crest.

Let us go back to the Severn for a final example of odd river behaviour, to an occurrence far surpassing that witnessed by the postman of Mickleham. At 4 am on the morning of 27 May 1773, a countryman living in a cottage at The Birches, between Buildwas and Coalbrookdale, was alarmed by a movement of the earth, saw a crack appearing in the ground, a field of oats heaving up and rolling about and the trees waving, although there was no wind. The waters of the river, then in flood, seemed to reverse towards their source. Then 'a great seam opened in the earth, running quickly upwards from the river; when 18 acres of land, with the trees and the hedges mostly standing, moved with great force and velocity towards the Severn, accompanied by a loud and uncommon noise'. A small wood fell into the river, whose current 'was thus forced, in large columns to a great height, driving the bed of the Severn to the opposite shore, where it lodged, more than 12 feet above the surface of low water, and, as it was supposed, 30 feet perpendicular above the bottom of the old channel.' Fish were left stranded and several barges were sunk. Nearly 400yd of turnpike road was displaced; the countryman's barn was thrown 35ft and destroyed while his house was moved 4ft but very little damaged.

Next day the Reverend John Fletcher, Vicar of Madeley, came to the spot to preach a sermon. He took his text from Numbers 16, referring to the men of Korah who fell into a pit opened up to receive them by the Lord. 'Go', he exhorted his congregation, 'to the ancient bank of the Severn. You come to it, and she is gone! You are in the middle of her old bed; nay, you cross it before you suspect that you have reached her shore: you stand in the deepest part of her channel, and yet you are in a wood! Large oaks spread their branches where bargemen unfurled their sails:—you walk to-day on solid ground where fishes yesterday swam in twenty feet of water. A rock that formed the bottom of the river has mounted up as a cork and gained a dry place on the bank, while a travelling grove has planted itself in the waters, and a fugitive river has invaded dry land.' Can anything be odder than that?

10

RIVERS TODAY AND TOMORROW

The setting up of Regional Water Authorities on 1 April 1974 was the most recent step to date in the long history of legislation concerning rivers. This legislation began in the thirteenth century with the relevant clauses in Magna Carta, the appointment of the first Commission of Sewers—for Romney Marsh in 1232—and the first Salmon Protection Act. Legislation in the following centuries was concerned mainly with individual rivers, as we have seen. With the growth of industries and the movement of people into large, densely housed communities, the problems of water supply became a national as well as a local concern. Although supply continued to be handled at a local level, by several hundred independent water companies, attempts were made by central government to tackle the damage caused by pollution, particularly after it was realised in 1831 that diseases such as cholera were waterborne. The Waterworks (Gasworks) Clauses Act of 1847 was in effect an anti-pollution measure, but neither this nor its several successors had much of an impact. One of the most effective actions in the nineteenth century was the establishment of the Geological Survey in 1835, which led to many major discoveries affecting water supply.

In 1930 the Land Drainage Act resulted in the setting up of Catchment Boards across the whole of England and Wales, with responsibility for controlling the flow of their designated main rivers and for improving the drainage in their areas. They were financed by a precept on the general rate and they were remarkably successful, on the whole, in the tasks allotted to them. Before the Catchment Boards, control of the navigable rivers in particular was a thing of shreds and patches. Only the Thames was under the control of a single body throughout its length. The Severn Commissioners were responsible for only 42 miles of the river and for none of its tributaries; the Humber's conservancy commission had nothing to do with the upkeep of its banks; the Trent's conservancy authority was a navigation company controlling 73 miles from Gainsborough upwards; the Medway and Warwickshire Avon were each divided between two authorities; the tidal stretch of the Nene came under eight different bodies, and no fewer than seventeen sets of commissioners were responsible for the Witham.

The Catchment Boards were supplanted by River Boards in 1948; these bodies had the added duty of preventing pollution. There were Rivers (Prevention of Pollution) Acts in 1951 and 1961, and a Tidal Waters Act in 1960. By the early 1960s pollution, through the efforts of both public and private bodies and their scientists and engineers, was on the way to being conquered. Attention turned to water supply, and in 1963 an Act established the Water Resources Board. In the following years this board, the supply companies and the River Authorities shared the control of water supplies, but 1,400 local authorities were still responsible for domestic sewage.

Following various reports, surveys and White Papers, the Water Act was passed in 1973. This set up a National Water Council and the Regional Water Authorities. In the words of the council's first chairman, Lord Nugent, 'The new structure . . . has given England and Wales probably the most advanced system of management of any country in the world. It has in effect unified the whole hydrological cycle of conservation, distribution and reclamation under one management. The new structure consists of 10 autonomous, multi-purpose Water Authorities and a National Water Council on which sit the 10 Regional Chairmen, to give co-ordination and leadership at national level. This compact structure replaces the former 29 River Authorities, 157 Water Undertakings (the 30 Water Companies are continuing as independent agents of WA's), and about 1,400 Sewage Authorities.'

In this splendid hydrological world, all the 'shallow brooks and rivers wide' have their place. England has nine water authorities: the North West, Northumbrian, Severn-Trent, Yorkshire, Anglian, Thames, Southern, Wessex and South West; and Wales has its National Water Development Authority, perhaps more euphonious in its native tongue—*Awdurdod Cenedlaethol Datblygu Dwr Cymru*. In the middle of all this is the British Waterways Board, guardians of most of the canal system and of the navigation of some rivers. BWB has no concern with any waterway in the Northumbrian, Southern or South West regions; in the other regions its mileage ranges from 824 in Severn-Trent to 64 in Wessex, and it also has responsibility for 135 miles of waterway in Scotland. Two government departments—Environment and Agricul-

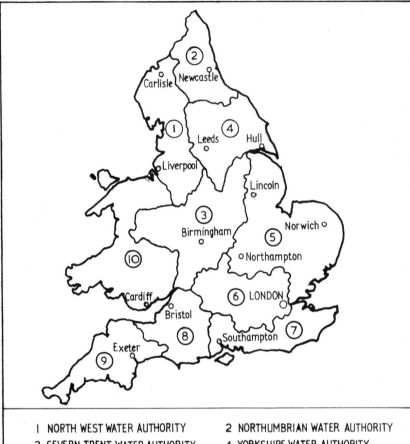

1 NORTH WEST WATER AUTHORITY	2 NORTHUMBRIAN WATER AUTHORITY
3 SEVERN-TRENT WATER AUTHORITY	4 YORKSHIRE WATER AUTHORITY
5 ANGLIAN WATER AUTHORITY	6 THAMES WATER AUTHORITY
7 SOUTHERN WATER AUTHORITY	8 WESSEX WATER AUTHORITY
9 SOUTH WEST WATER AUTHORITY	10 WELSH NATIONAL WATER DEVELOPMENT AUTHORITY

The Regional Water Authorities of England and Wales, created by the Water Act of 1973. They superseded 29 river authorities, 157 water boards and 1,393 local sewerage and sewage disposal undertakings. They also inherited debts of £2,400 million. The areas they service range from the 3,549 square miles of the Northumbrian WA to the 10,563 of the Anglian WA. The Thames WA, with nearly 12 million living in its area, serves the largest population.

ture, Fisheries and Food—are involved; there are also two bodies concerned with the non-industrial use of water, the Water Space Amenity Commission and the Inland Waterways Amenity Advisory Council. In addition there is a vast number of voluntary organisations partly or wholly concerned with waterways, such as the National Trust, the RSPB and the National Conservation Corps, whose interests cover the whole country, or the Inland Waterways Association, whose main preoccupation is with the maintenance and improvement of navigation on canals and rivers, or the Great Ouse Restoration Society, founded with the aim of restoring the navigation of that river to Bedford. And then there are the angling clubs, the sailing clubs, the rowing clubs, the cruising clubs; organisations for those who water-ski or sub-aqua dive or wish to preserve, conserve or observe. It is all enormously impressive. Whatever, one wonders, would 'the great god Pan, down in the reeds by the river' make of it all?

Before he made up his mind, he ought to look more closely at the work of the key unit, as far as rivers are concerned—the Regional Water Authority. Each RWA has a chairman, appointed by the Environment Secretary, a number of members depending on its area and the population served—Thames has fifty-seven, the North West twenty-seven—appointed by the government departments involved and the county and district councils, and a headquarters staff led by a chief executive and with directors of various departments—Anglian has directors of Resource Planning, Operations, Scientific Services, Finance and Administration. Not all RWAs are organised in the same way; Anglian has 5 river divisions, 8 water divisions and 7 sewage divisions, while Southern has 9 single or dual purpose divisions. Then there are committees, advisory committees, councils, panels; in short, RWAs are great bureaucratic machines, employing thousands of people; Yorkshire WA, covering roughly the old county of Yorkshire, employs almost 6,000, and South West, one of the smallest, over 2,000.

The role of a Water Authority is summed up in the words of the Yorkshire WA in its guide to services (the coincidence of this authority with a county traditionally conscious of its own identity must be the reason for the threefold repetition of the name in the first sentence). 'The Yorkshire Water Authority's essential duty is to care for the well-being of the rivers of Yorkshire for their use and enjoyment by the people of Yorkshire. To this end we build, maintain and operate engineering works to supply and recover water, control flows into sewers, to alleviate floodings, to control abstractions from and discharges into rivers, operate compensation water, manage water quality, and also conserve fisheries and amenities and manage the facilities for angling and water recreation. We provide all the water you need at the twist of a tap. . . .' The budget for this authority for 1976/7 was over £103 million. The Thames WA budget for the same year was nearly three times as much, at £287 million, while a small authority, the South West, handled £54 million.

The Water Authorities were unfortunate in that, shortly after their creation, the national economy took a sharp turn for the worse. The general public, not quite so convinced, as they once seemed to be, that bigger necessarily means better, looked somewhat askance at the new offices and the new hierarchy. The RWAs seemed to feel unloved; they felt the Press was not always kind to them, and the attempts of some to improve their image by allocating more funds to public and press relations did not, when duly publicised, make matters any better. Geographically and emotionally the Yorkshire WA might seem to make some sense; but what could one make of an organisation responsible for all the rivers from north Lincolnshire to south Essex with its headquarters in offices in Huntingdon? Did its chief officers even know where all its rivers were?

Well, by now presumably they do; in any event, we are, for the time being, committed to this form of organisation and must learn to live with it. It is too soon to evaluate the performance of the RWAs in general and it would be unfair to try to do so. But it is fair to point out that mistakes have been made; for example, the Anglian Authority's refusal to accept the arguments of the Inland Waterways Association and the River Stour Trust on certain clauses of its Private Bill, resulting in a petition heard by a Special Committee of the House of Lords which decided against the authority. One hopes that the authorities will learn from experience, will pay more than mere lip-service to the principle of consultation, and will have room at the top for men of the calibre, say, of George Dallas of the old Nene Catchment Board, with similar vision, energy and understanding.

More perhaps than any other feature of the landscape, rivers engender emotion. People love rivers; perhaps the day will come when they will also love Water Authorities. But—such is the way of things—that day may not come until the Water Authorities themselves are in danger of being replaced by some other form of organisation; there are strong men who may still be weeping for the loss of the old Thames Conservancy, as there are many boaters who are fighting for the retention of their old enemy, the British Waterways Board.

One operation which has been met with universal praise and pleasure has been the cleansing of the tidal Thames, the result of the combined efforts of a number of bodies, including the Conservancy, the Port of London Authority, the LCC, the Metropolitan Water Board, industrialists, local councils and others. Now the responsibility for the condition of the river wholly belongs to the Thames Water Authority under whose aegis the task is being brought to completion. It is estimated that the purification of the river cost about £100 million over the years; and, so greatly have costs risen, this is the same figure that is being quoted for the cleansing of the much smaller estuary of the Tyne. The authority facing the worst pollution problems at the present time is the North West, which reckons that about 25 per cent of the country's highly polluted watercourses are within its area, including the notorious Tame. To purify the Tame will be an expensive and lengthy task, but there is no doubt that in time it will be done. Indeed, for the problems of pollution, and of water supply, the RWAs may prove themselves the best fitted of organisations to find the answers. The long, hot summer of 1976 did more than spoil the sport of anglers or necessitate the closure of locks; it showed how vulnerable England and Wales are in periods of prolonged drought and how much needs to be done both in increasing the reserves of water available and in educating the public to conserve this element usually taken for granted, but suddenly so precious.

Feelings run highest, however, when the recreational use of rivers is discussed. How can the interests of all those who seek pleasure from our rivers be reconciled? Fishermen accuse boaters of polluting the rivers and disturbing their sport; ornithologists accuse fishermen of discarding nylon line, hooks and weights, which can maim or destroy birds; speed-boats and water-skiers are detested by all except their owners and themselves; botanists look with suspicion at the clumsy feet of everyone else; and so it goes on. The Yorkshire WA puts the problem very gently when it says that its plan 'is to see that Yorkshire waters serve all the recreational uses for which they are suitable. With proper goodwill towards bankside owners and among themselves, anglers, boaters, picknickers and ramblers will find enjoyment in or beside the waters of the area in the years ahead'. Presumably they did so in the past as well; the rivers were there long before the authority. But now leisure itself has become a kind of industry. For the year 1974/5 the Anglian Authority issued over 400,000 fishing licences, while there were about 20,000 vessels registered in its area, more than half of them on the Broads. It is not surprising that this and other authorities show no enthusiasm when mention is made of the possibility of reintroducing commercial

Normanton Church, preserved as a memorial to the County of Rutland, much of which has been submerged beneath Rutland Water

navigation, which they would see as adding far more to their problems than it would to their revenue.

How then can we sum up the present situation? There are signs of a growing awareness of the fragility of our heritage, and architects and engineers are showing a sensitivity which seemed to have disappeared in the brutalist approach of a few years ago—for evidence see the treatment of new reservoirs, of which Rutland Water is an example. Despite pleas that a concrete path be built through Dovedale, such a path has not been built, and somehow the beauty of the riverside survives despite the hundreds of thousands of visitors who descend on it in the summer months. Symond's Yat on the Wye, High Force on the Tees, Dedham and Flatford Mill on the Stour—each year they attract more and more tourists but who is to say that they have suffered therefrom? The living water and its environment may resist the impress of man better than the summit of Snowdon or the stones of Stonehenge. And, in the sphere of recreation, although interests conflict and will continue to do so, there is space enough for everyone, as long as everyone does not try to occupy the same space at the same time. The boater may be using his craft as a GRP weekend cottage; the angler may merely be escaping from his wife and children; who knows what frustrations of civilisation may drive men to pursuits by the riverside that to others may seem strange and unaccountable? The spiritual and mental re-creation that rivers may provide can be as valuable to the individual as their more obvious utilitarian functions.

In towns and cities too there is a new awareness of the value of the river. Thetford is an example of a small town which, in expanding, has treated its river, the Little Ouse, with care and sensitivity. Both Peterborough and Northampton have paid more respect to the Nene in recent years than they did in the past, providing riverside walks through parkland and plenty of moorings for boats. Stratford's Avon has become more interesting and more useful since the navigation was reopened and the new lock installed. Cambridge is realising that there is more to the Cam than the famous Backs and its planners have produced a model report on the river and its immediate surroundings. Glasgow is paying more attention to the amenity value of the Clyde and to the quality of the buildings on the riverside. And the same can be said of several other major cities, although nothing can be done about the substantial horrors built on the riversides earlier this century, of which the south bank of the Thames in London provides some of the most notorious examples.

Finally there should be a word or two about the future. The major engineering project now in progress is the building of the Thames Barrier in Woolwich Reach, due for completion in 1981. With the slow but gradual sinking of the south east of England and the rising of the tide levels, the dangers of flooding have increased. With a 'surge tide', such as occurred in 1953, and high winds, the risk is great. Raising the banks is one way of preventing flooding and they have been raised twice in the last fifty years, but there is a limit to this method of defence. The protective measure eventually chosen was the barrier. A number of piers are being built across the river, each containing machinery for raising gates between them. The gates are housed in casings on the bed of the river and can be swung up into position in about fifteen minutes. In normal circumstances, therefore, the only obstructions in the river will be the piers themselves. Four of the openings will be 200ft wide, two of them 100ft, and there will be narrower gaps for light craft. Hence navigation will not be impeded. The barrier is being built for the future when, as the possibility of flooding increases, it will be necessary for the protection of the low-lying areas of London. In the past, London has been flooded several times; in 1236 men were rowing in Westminster Hall, in 1663 Whitehall was under water after what Samuel Pepys described as 'the greatest tide that ever was remembered in England', and in 1928 fourteen people were drowned in central areas. Had the great floods of 1953 reached London the disaster would have been unimaginable.

The barrier will be the largest of its kind in the world. Each gate is designed to withstand a load of more than 9,000 tonnes and the whole structure should protect the million or so people living and working in the lower-lying area of Greater London. Below the barrier safety will be ensured by wall and embankment raising and strengthening. The cost of the barrier and the associated works above it is likely to be of the order of £200 million.

Another large-scale undertaking, due to be completed in 1980, is the Kielder Water Scheme in north Northumberland. Two dams across the north Tyne will create a large reservoir with a surface area of 2,684 acres and a storage capacity of 41,350 million gallons. Work began in 1974, and the new road to replace the Yarrowmoor-Kielder road, which will be submerged by the reservoir, was opened in September 1977. From the reservoir the flow of water down the Tyne will be regulated; in addition, water will be transferred from Riding Mill on the Tyne through tunnels to outlets on the Wear and Tees, a total distance of 24 miles. The Northumbrian Water Authority reckons that the Kielder scheme will safeguard the water supplies in its area until 2001.

In 1971 work began on investigating the feasibility of storing water in the Wash. Many experiments have taken place and much data has been collected but, as the predicted costs continue to rise and the difficulties accumulate, it seems unlikely that a Wash Barrage will be constructed in the foreseeable future. Similarly the imaginative scheme proposed by the Inland Shipping Group for a new watercourse from the Wash to a point south of Birmingham and thence to the Severn, to be used for water transfer and supply as well as for navigation, seems to have little hope of realisation for many decades at least.

It seems probable, then, that the immediate future will see the continuation of projects already in hand—a few of which, like the extending and improving of training banks at the outfalls of some of the major east coast rivers, have been in hand for over a century—but that nothing really large-scale or dramatic is likely to be launched. There will be development and extension of water transfer schemes and it is likely that more stretches of countryside will disappear under new reservoirs, especially if the campaign to make the public more aware of the value of water and less prodigal in its use is not successful. The dirtier rivers will be cleaned up and, with the increasing demand on water space for recreational use, we must expect to see more regulations and restrictions.

I would like to hope that not everything on every riverside will be labelled, categorised, zoned or tamed into submission. There must be room for 'wildness and wet' as well as for notices reserving angling for members of a particular club, or pump-out stations for pleasure craft. And, while we applaud the return of life to the Thames and other rivers, it is the life of fish, birds and plants we are talking about, not the life of men. Those who used to gain their livelihood from the rivers, manning the trading vessels, working on the now deserted wharves and in the now crumbling warehouses—will their kind ever return? Playgrounds, bath-fillers, habitats, drains—our rivers are all these. But is that all that we want them to be?

APPENDIX

THE PRINCIPAL RIVERS OF ENGLAND AND
WALES

Extracted from Appendix B of the *Report of the Select Committee of
the House of Lords on Conservancy Boards*, 1877, pp 282-6

I

FIRST-CLASS RIVERS HAVING CATCHMENT BASINS OF 1000 SQUARE
MILES AND UPWARDS

	Name	County	Length in Miles	Area of Basin (sq miles)	Tributaries Number	Tributaries Length (united)
1	Humber	York	37	1229	2	55
2	Mersey	Lancaster	68	1707	6	188
3	Nene	Northants	99	1055	1	11
4	Ouse	York	59½	4207	11	629
5	Ouse	Camb. and Beds	156¼	2894	8	212
6	Severn	Gloucester	178	4437	17	450
7	Thames	Gloucester	201¼	5162	15	463
8	Trent	Lincoln	167½	3543	10	293
9	Tyne	Northumb'land	35	1053	6	154
10	Witham	Lincoln	89	1052	4	75
11	Wye	Hereford	148	1655	9	223

SECOND-CLASS RIVERS HAVING CATCHMENT BASINS OF FROM 500 TO 1000 SQUARE MILES

	Name	County	Length in Miles	Area of Basin (sq miles)	Tributaries	
					Number	Length (united)
1	Avon	Somerset	78½	869	4	59
2	Avon	Hants	67	666	1	28¼
3	Dee	Flint	93	850	4	82
4	Eden	Cumberland	79½	916	4	97½
5	Exe	Devon	58½	562	5	81¼
6	Medway	Kent	69	997	3	62½
7	Parrett	Somerset	38½	561	4	106
8	Ribble	Lancaster	61	501	4	90¾
9	Tees	York	95	744	9	132
10	Test	Hants	35¼	544	1	6¾
11	Towy	Carmarthen	66½	522	3	55
12	Usk	Mon	76½	650	7	107
13	Welland	Northants	72½	707	3	78
14	Yare	Norfolk	35	553	4	84

III

THIRD-CLASS RIVERS HAVING CATCHMENT BASINS OF FROM 100 TO 500 SQUARE MILES

	Name	County	Length in Miles	Area of Basin (sq miles)	Tributaries	
					Number	Length (united)
1	Adur	Sussex	21	147	—	—
2	Alde	Suffolk	30¾	127	1	8
3	Aln	Northumb'land	24	102	—	—
4	Alt	Lancaster	16½	170	—	—
5	Arun	Sussex	51½	349	—	—
6	Axe	Devon	25¼	155	1	14½
7	Blackwater	Essex	50	465	2	53
8	Brue	Somerset	36¼	197	—	—
9	Bure	Norfolk	52¼	338	1	11¼
10	Camel	Cornwall	28¼	155	1	8¼

	Name	County	Length in Miles	Area of Basin (sq miles)	Tributaries Number	Tributaries Length (united)
11	Cleddau, W	Pembroke	24½	116	—	—
12	Colne	Essex	37¾	200	1	13¼
13	Conway	Carnarvon	30¼	224	3	29¾
14	Coquet	Northumb'land	45	213	—	—
15	Crouch	Essex	20½	150	1	13¼
16	Dart	Devon	37¼	179	1	10½
17	Deben	Suffolk	32	159	1	10
18	Derwent	Cumberland	35¼	268	1	13½
19	Derwent	Derby	64¼	429	3	37
20	Dovey	Montgomery	35	264	5	44½
21	Duddon	Cumberland	27¼	117	—	—
22	Elwy	Denbigh	31½	306	3	49¾
23	Esk	Cumberland	8¼	143	2	35
24	Esk	York	29½	136	3	25
25	Fal	Cornwall	30½	118	1	9¼
26	Fowey	Cornwall	27	116	1	6¼
27	Frome	Dorset	34	206	1	7¾
28	Glaslyn	Carnarvon	18½	142	1	14¾
29	Itchen	Hants	27¼	137	—	—
30	Kent	Cumberland	28½	196	4	49
31	Leven	Lancaster	6½	123	3	25
32	Llwchwr	Carmarthen	22½	130	5	45
33	Lune	Lancaster	53½	434	3	41¼
34	Mawddach	Merioneth	21¼	147	3	26¼
35	Neath	Glamorgan	24½	121	3	23½
36	Ogmore	Glamorgan	15¾	111	3	27¾
37	Orwell	Suffolk	35	257	—	—
38	Ouse	Sussex	34¼	212	—	—
39	Portsmouth and Chichester Basin	Sussex	—	315	—	—
40	Rother	Sussex	33½	281	—	—
41	Steeping	Lincoln	24	102	—	—
42	Stour	Essex	61¾	420	2	34
43	Stour (Gt)	Kent	52¾	291	1	12
44	Stour	Dorset	64	479	2	25
45	Taf	Carmarthen	31¾	187	2	27
46	Taf	Glamorgan	38¼	202	6	59¼
47	Tamar	Cornwall	35¾	381	2	32
48	Teign	Devon	34½	189	—	—

					Tributaries	
49	Titchfield	Hants	20¾	128	—	—
50	Torridge	Devon	52½	349	2	30
51	Towy	Glamorgan	27¼	110	1	10½
52	Trent	Dorset	21½	125	—	—
53	Tweed	Northumb'land	22	267	1	30
54	Wansbeck	Northumb'land	27	183	2	27½
55	Waveney	Norfolk	58¾	339	—	—
56	Wear	Durham	70	455	6	76¾
57	Wyre	Lancaster	35¼	179	2	20¼
58	Yeo	Somerset	14¼	127	—	—

IV

FOURTH-CLASS RIVERS HAVING CATCHMENT BASINS OF FROM 50 TO 100 SQUARE MILES

	Name	County	Length in Miles	Area of Basin (sq miles)	Tributaries	
					Number	Length (united)
1	Aeron	Cardigan	19½	63	—	—
2	Avon	Devon	23¼	55	—	—
3	Ax	Somerset	24	98	—	—
4	Blyth	Northumb'land	26½	80	1	19¼
5	Blythe	Suffolk	18¼	71	—	—
6	Cleddau (E)	Pembroke	19½	80	1	12¾
7	Cuckmere	Sussex	24	75	—	—
8	Duncleddau	Pembroke	11	76	—	—
9	Dysynni	Merioneth	14	64	—	—
10	Ehen	Cumberland	14½	59	—	—
11	Ellen	Cumberland	20¾	54	—	—
12	Ereh	Carnarvon	12	53	—	—
13	Germain, St	Cornwall	8	95	2	35½
14	Lac or Ely	Glamorgan	24	64	—	—
15	Line Water	Northumb'land	15½	50	—	—
16	Otter	Devon	27	95	—	—
17	Plym	Devon	15	73	—	—
18	Rheidol	Cardigan	25½	74	2	32
19	Rumney	Glamorgan	35½	99	1	7
20	Tavey	Devon	23	87	1	12
21	Taw	Devon	48¾	77	3	49½
22	Wampool	Cumberland	18	62	1	8
23	Withern	Lincoln	20¼	91	—	—
24	Ystwyth	Cardigan	23¼	75	—	—

V

This class contains 143 rivers, the length of which varies from 19¾ miles—Tetney Drain, in Lincolnshire, the basin of which has an area of 44 square miles—to 2 miles (the Sillybrook, in Glamorganshire, the basis of which has an area of 19 square miles); and 22 of them are apparently nameless, as they are described simply as streams.

PRINCIPAL RIVERS AND STREAMS OF SCOTLAND

Extracted from Groome's *Ordnance Gazetteer of Scotland,* new edition, vol iii, p 515

Name	Area of Basin in sq miles	Tributaries	Length of Course in miles
Tay	2400		$119\frac{3}{8}$
		Bran	19
		Almond	30
		Earn	$46\frac{1}{4}$
		Lyon	$34\frac{1}{4}$
		Tummel	29
		Garry	22
		Tilt	$15\frac{3}{8}$
		Isla	37
Tweed	1870		97
		Ettrick	$32\frac{5}{8}$
		Yarrow	$14\frac{1}{2}$
		Teviot	$37\frac{1}{4}$
		Jed	$21\frac{3}{4}$
		Tili	40
		Bowmont	20
		Lyne	$18\frac{3}{4}$
		Eddleston	9
		Gala Water	21
		Lauder or Leader	$21\frac{1}{4}$
		Whiteadder	34

Name	Area of Basin in sq miles	Tributaries	Length of Course in miles
Clyde	1480		106
		Medwin	15
		Calder	10
		Kelvin	21
		Leven	$7\frac{1}{4}$
		Douglas	20
		Avon	$24\frac{1}{4}$
		Cart	19
		Irvine	$29\frac{1}{2}$
		Annick	16
		Garnock	$21\frac{1}{8}$
		Cessnock	14
Spey	1190		96
		Avon	$27\frac{3}{4}$
		Dulnain	28
Dee (Aberdeenshire)	700		$87\frac{1}{8}$
Forth	645		$116\frac{1}{2}$
		Bannock Burn	14
		Carron	20
		Leith, Water of	24
		South Esk	23
		North Esk	17
		Teith	34
		Allan	20
		Devon	$33\frac{3}{4}$
		Leven	16
		Ore	17
Don	530		$82\frac{1}{4}$
		Ury	18
Beauly	324		40
		Cannich	24
		Farrer	$27\frac{1}{2}$
Oikell	300		$35\frac{1}{4}$
		Carron	9
		Shin	$7\frac{5}{8}$

Name	Length	Name	Length
Nith	$70\frac{3}{4}$	Ayr	38
Scar	$18\frac{3}{8}$		
Cluden	23	Lugar	$12\frac{1}{2}$
		Eden	$29\frac{1}{2}$
Annan	49	South Esk	29
Evan	$16\frac{1}{4}$	Doon	$26\frac{1}{2}$
Ae	16	Findhorn	$62\frac{1}{4}$
Moffat Water	14	Deveron	$61\frac{5}{8}$
Milk Water	$17\frac{3}{4}$	Nairn	38
		Ythan	$35\frac{1}{8}$
Esk	$36\frac{3}{4}$	Helmsdale	$27\frac{1}{2}$
		Thurso	27
Ewes	$11\frac{3}{4}$	Naver	$18\frac{7}{8}$
Tarras	11	Conan	$12\frac{1}{4}$
Liddel	$26\frac{3}{4}$		
North Esk	$48\frac{3}{4}$		
Dee (Kirkcudbright)	$38\frac{1}{2}$		
Ken	$28\frac{1}{2}$		

INDEX

205

207